The Mind Diet Hype

"Edwina has helped me change my body. *The Mind Diet* will help you change yours."
Dr. Mike Dow, NY Times Bestselling Author, *The Brain Fog Fix*

"Edwina been my sports nutritionist for numerous winning title fights. It's great to see the mindset and methodology we used everyday put into a book that everyone can benefit from."
Quinton "Rampage" Jackson, *Former UFC Light Heavyweight Champion*, Mixed Martial Artist and Actor

"Over the last year, Edwina's "mind-body" tools have helped me write a new story about who I am when it comes to health and fitness. The force of her incredibly positive attitude and her smarts comes through every page of this book. Read it. Edwina Cheer is the real deal!"
Tracy Poust, Emmy Award-winning Writer/Executive Producer
Will & Grace, Ugly Betty

"*The Mind Diet* is a perfect supplementary tool for a person to the achieve their optimal level of health. In health, mindset is everything!"
Craig Ramsay, Celebrity Fitness Expert/Television Personality

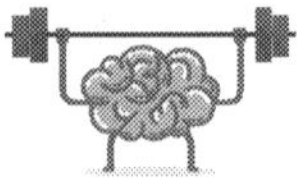

The Mind Diet Hype

"*The Mind Diet* is a must read for anyone who is ready to live their lives at their greatest level of health!"
Luke Milton, Founder *Training Mate,* Pro Australian Rugby/ NRL Player

"*The Mind Diet* does a great job at teaching you the importance of mental wellbeing and how instrumental it is to achieving and maintaining your health and fitness goals."
Mike Donavanik, CSCS, Celebrity Personal Trainer

"*The Mind Diet* is the ultimate motivational tool for achieving your health and fitness goals."
Tahndi Campbell, Executive Director, *BeFiT Channel, Lionsgate Ent.*
Owner, *Pavement City*

"Edwina is my go-to fitness guru, and *The Mind Diet* has proven to be an invaluable guide for our regular training sessions. I'm thrilled readers worldwide can now access and benefit from *The Mind Diet* program."
Andrew Strauser, Head of Unscripted, *Jennifer Lopez Ent, Nuyorican Prod.*

The Mind Diet Hype

"*The Mind Diet* is the best combo of "real talk," self help and humor, and is like getting to take Edwina with you everywhere in your pocket. Like even on an airplane, but I don't have to buy her an actual plane ticket…"
Tom Lenk, Actor, *Buffy The Vampire Slayer, Angel, #LenkLewk E! Network*

"I've been lucky enough to have been trained by, and trained alongside Edwina. She is truly the mental and physical embodiment of all that she teaches in *The Mind Diet.* A laser beam of positivity!"
Dan MacPherson, Australian Film and TV Actor, *Strike Back, APB, The Shannnara Chronicles*

"*The Mind Diet* is a must-read for anyone who is not getting the results they want following other diets and programs, but not knowing why!"
Jonathan Bennett, Actor and Host, *Mean Girls, Dancing With The Stars*

Solar Publishing Ltd.

ISBN-10:0-692-80016-6
ISBN-13:978-0-692-80016-4

For information on special discounts or bulk purchases:

Solar Publishing Pty. Ltd

7119 W. Sunset Blvd

Suite 716

Los Angeles, CA 90046

For all other general enquiries please email gday@mindandbodydiet.com

Disclaimer

The Mind Diet is written and created by Celebrity Sports Nutritionist Edwina Cheer. *The Mind Diet* twelve step guide provides general services and program advice for improving the health and wellness of individuals only. *The Mind Diet* is not to be considered as a substitute or replacement plan in lieu of medical advice, treatment or psychotherapy. Products, services, and *The Mind Diet* guides are not intended to diagnose, treat, cure, or prevent disease. Please consult with a physician or appropriate medical professional before beginning any exercise or nutrition program.

Statements made within *The Mind Diet* guides in respect to products, supplements and opinions have not been evaluated by the Food and Drug Administration. *The Mind Diet* and Solar Publishing Pty. Ltd make no warranties regarding the completeness, accuracy or timeliness of the information within *The Mind Diet.*

The reader acknowledges and agrees *The Mind Diet* and supporting intermediaries including Solar Publishing Pty. Ltd and Eddsthetics LLC shall not be responsible or liable, directly or indirectly, for any damage or loss caused or allegedly claimed to be caused by, or in connection with an individual's misuse of *The Mind Diet* guides and supplementary programs.

The Mind Diet

For Maria Cheer, *'my why'*

and

For you.

Helping you is what I came to Earth to do.

CONTENTS

Introduction

Oh goody! Another weight loss book. Another fad diet trend that promises you the moon, where you'll either need to drink some crazy concoction of lemon and cayenne pepper, ingest no carbohydrates for the rest of your life, or live on no sugar (and essentially no fun), till the end of time.

Perhaps you've already tried it all, and none of them work. Or maybe the fad diets and workouts are good for a short period of time, but a few months to a year down the track you're back where you started (or in even worse shape than you were originally). I can understand your skepticism. To put the icing on the cake, many of these trends have worked for some people. People are claiming to get results, but why not you? What gives?

The Mind Diet

Generally speaking, many of the diet or exercise trends you may have seen are not bad diets or programs. Many of them do what they claim to do. However, nearly all of these trends are missing something. They address the physical, but fail to address the mental wellbeing of a person. Being mentally fit is a foundation whereby from which all of these diets can be successfully executed. Simply put, for long term lasting success in fitness and health, it is integral that your mental fitness game has its own workout program too.

Introducing The Mind Diet.

The Mind Diet can be combined with any diet and exercise program currently existing to you. Vegan, Paleo, bodybuilders, CrossFit, pescetarians, and everything in between! In fact, not implementing **The Mind Diet** in conjunction with your health and fitness program is your one cheat-meal ticket to fitness failure. It is the brick and mortar you will need to build your sustainable and ideal fitness body… and also a game plan that is useful in your relationships, career and spiritual practice.

Follow this guide in an honest fashion, and you'll find yourself bursting through fitness plateaus, saying hello to your dream level of health, and the best part: being able to use **The Mind Diet** not only for your fitness goals, but for progression and success in all other areas of your life.

Are you ready?

The Mind Diet Guide	
STEP 1A	DEFINE YOUR FITNESS UTOPIA/BIG WHAT
STEP 1B	DEFINE YOUR LITTLE WHATS
STEP 2A	DEFINE BIG WHY
STEP 2B	DEFINE LITTLE WHY
STEP 3A	CREATE A DEADLINE FOR FITNESS UTOPIA
STEP 3B	DEFINE LITTLE D'S
STEP 4	JUMP!
STEP 5	DEPLOY MUSCLE UPS (BECOME BFFS WITH FAILURE)
STEP 6	CREATE THE HABIT
STEP 7	FIND YOUR STRENGTH IN THE SPECIFICS
STEP 8A	SAY NO
STEP 8B	LET GO
STEP 9	CREATE YOUR SPACE OF CHEER
STEP 10	RUN YOUR OWN RACE
STEP 11	FINISH WHAT YOU STARTED
STEP 12	GIVE IT AWAY

Chapter 1

What Do You Want?

I can teach anybody how to get what they want out of life. The problem is that I can't find anybody who can tell me what they want.
- Mark Twain

Have you ever seen the movie, *The Notebook?* There is a famous scene in it where a mill worker called Noah, played by Ryan Reynolds - and a rich girl Allie, played by Rachel McAdams are the main characters in a passionate love story. Allie, the belle of the ball, is being forced to choose between two men. Oh, to be Allie! The dashing, "perfect on paper" man she is engaged to be married to, or the humble, artistic but romantically broke Noah, who in truth she is in love with.

In the scene, Noah asks Allie repeatedly, "What do you want? What do you want? DAMMIT, WHAT DO YOU WANT?" Allie is looking quite the damsel in distress, shaking her head at him, not really knowing what to say. After some arduous moments of her spluttering near tears, shaking her head (at which point I could have honestly strangled her if I could have), she says, "It's not that simple."

And the very simple reason why she has said, "it's not that simple," is that up until that point, she has not decided on her answer to a simple, yet incredibly difficult question for most humans. Luckily, this is movie world and she ends up making a decision. Once she makes this decision, the Universe is now clear what it is she is asking for and Noah and Allie sail off happily into the sunset.

Yeah, yeah, I get it. This is movie world. It's not real life. This may be the case, however some fundamental laws that exist in that film also exist in your own life today.

The Deal

I have had the pleasure of training many different types of individuals for fitness, health & nutrition. Whenever I start working with a new client, the first thing I always ask them is, "What do you want to achieve? Describe it."

These are invariably the answers I receive:

"I want to lose weight."
"I want to tone up."
"I want to look good for my wedding."
"I want to put on some muscle."
"I want to be healthier."
"I want to be tighter."

Maybe you see some of your own goals in these sentences. Perhaps that's the whole reason you're reading this, hoping to find some secret answer to your fitness success. Well, you're in luck! Here it is:

WHAT DO YOU WANT, DAMMIT?

Imagine I am Noah from *The Notebook*. I'm standing in front you, shaking you senseless, asking you this. Because through the cosmos, that's exactly what I am doing. "But I have!" you may say. "I want to lose weight." Well, what number exactly do you want to ideally be when you step onto the scale? Do you have a picture of your goal when you used to be that way, or a picture of someone you are working towards? Is it in front of you, somewhere that you can see it often (if not *all* of the time), instead of tucked away in some shoebox in the closet or worse - hidden away in the depths of your mind with the rest of your "I'll get to it someday" goals? Do you have the exact number of pounds or kilograms you would like to lose?

> **Many people don't get what they want from the Universe because it is simply unclear what it is that they are asking for.**
> **- Paul Meyer**

Although the answers above are great starting places, we cannot achieve what we want to achieve unless we **get**

specific about what it is. General fitness goals lead to general fitness results. These are less likely to stick around in the long run, because they are just "generally" around. And if you don't know where you're going, how do you know when you're there? #DuhBecky, you don't! This is one of the fundamental reasons why so many people cannot maintain their health and fitness in the long term.

Step 1a: Define Your Fitness Utopia

A goal properly set is halfway reached.
- Zig Ziglar, Motivational Speaker

Shake it off, people! Today is a new day and the world is your oyster. We begin our first step of **The Mind Diet** by thinking of the end in mind.

It's time to take responsibility for your health and fitness by getting super clear about what you want. This can be referred to as **The Big What, Big W**, one of the W's in your **3W** (more on that later), or your **Fitness Utopia**.

Your **Fitness Utopia** can be defined as the ultimate level that you can imagine yourself at in fitness and in health. The person within you that just can't get any better.

How The Mind Diet Works

As Chief Designer of your individually and fantastically created **Fitness Utopia,** and also Chief Programmer of your entire ***Mind Diet*** Program, you'll see many examples of mental exercises; or what are called **"Mind Diet Mental Moves"** in this book. Like a toolbox, consider them tools or tactics that you can choose to add into your very own **Mind Diet** program to best help you succeed.

Similar to a personal trainer or a nutritionist programming an exercise plan with different exercises, you will also be programming your very own **Mind Diet** program to work in conjunction with whatever exercise discipline or plan of eating that you have chosen.

Just as your physical self is different from that of your neighbor, partner, or random person sitting next to you at the coffee shop, we are all fabulously individual and worthy creatures that have slightly different triggers, fitness goals and fitness levels. To create your ideal **Fitness Utopia** and to follow the all of the 12 steps in **The Mind Diet** successfully**,** you will need to explore and experience each of the exercises listed throughout this book and discover which of ***The Mind Diet's Mental Moves*** work best for you. This includes deciding your ratio splits and frequency of these mental moves throughout the week. We will learn more about scheduling this later on, but the ultimate goal is to have **The Mind Diet** and the relevant exercises trigger or keep you in a forward moving frequency. A frequency that facilitates moving towards your specifically designed **Fitness Utopia** in the most efficient manner possible.

So relax, settle in and stay open to the possibility of a life changing transformation - you just might surprise yourself!

The Mind Diet Mental Moves

On Fitness Utopia Creation and Manifestation

Complete the following exercises below to aid in your discovery of choosing what your **Fitness Utopia** will look like.

The Fitness Utopia Mirror

Find yourself a quiet place, close your eyes and take a moment to center yourself. Then, imagine you are walking up to a bright, full-length mirror with gold trimming around the edges.

You look into the mirror. Standing there, staring back at you is the healthiest, highest and best version of yourself. What does he or she look like? Spare no detail. What do they have on?

Are they smiling? Are they talking to you? What are they saying? Have a conversation with them. Do they have any advice for you? Is there anyone around them? Where are they? This exercise should take about 15 minutes.

Afterwards, take some time to reflect on what you saw in the mirror. It may not be the **Fitness Utopia** you decide on completely, but it's a great exercise and it's fun to see what the limits of your mind show you. Are you entertaining the possibilities of your greatness? Do you truly believe these things can come to pass?

I find it beneficial to journal or write these things down while it's still fresh in your mind. It's also beneficial to log how you feel about the differences between where you might be right now, and where you want to go.

The Balloon Drop

This exercise involves purchasing some helium balloons. Can you think of any toxic habits that hinder your journey to your **Fitness Utopia?** Write them down on each balloon. If you are with a friend or group, sit with each balloon and talk about how this has stopped you from stepping into your best self, why you think it has and how this has made you feel. Then when you are ready, release the balloon and watch it fly away.

Although this exercise and it's benefits are talked about in detail in Chapter 7, however at this preliminary stage of **The Mind Diet**, it is still a great exercise to begin with and keep in your program throughout your journey!

The Vision Board

A vision board is one of the tried and true exercises of the self help world. It can be a great tool to help clarify and maintain focus towards a specific fitness goal.

What you include in your vision board is based on your own triggers that ultimately motivate you into action. They can include photos, affirmations, a list of past successes, and really anything that elevates your frequency and helps you to move towards your **Fitness Utopia**.

A Tip On Designing Your Fitness Utopia

Design is not just what it looks like and feels like. Design is how it works.
Steve Jobs

So back to Step 1a: When designing your **Fitness Utopia**, I encourage you to take note of one of my favorite quotes from Steve Jobs. Jobs is known as one of the biggest technology designers and innovators of our time. His statement holds true for any type of good design, including creating the functionally fabulous design that you are calling your **Fitness Utopia**. Just as Jobs has created many life changing and innovative ways for the world to connect and interact, you are the designer of your life and are also able to change the design and function of your body (and ultimately your whole life) in a manner that can be just as innovative as any of the creations we've seen from Apple.

Through being in the health and fitness industry and being a fitness competitor, I have definitely seen some extreme ends of the spectrum in my time. My advice to you when designing your **Fitness Utopia**: Aim for your design to function as well as it looks.

By function, I mean not only anatomically, but also functional for your life and lifestyle. This does not mean I am against extreme ends of sports. If you are a professional bodybuilder who makes a living in professional competition or that's what your dream is, then yes - the body of Mr Olympia is very functional to you and I think it's a wonderful **Fitness Utopia** to have. However, if you are Joe Blow or Becky Big Booty who works in telemarketing, choosing to design a body like Mr/Ms Olympia is clearly not functional for your life and therefore poor design on your part.

Good design means taking the steps to design your body and also your entire life so it functions as well as it looks. What is the value in working your ass to the bone as a stockbroker, if you end up with a stress related heart attack at 40 years old, and can't enjoy the fruits of your labor? Similarly, what is the point of carving your body into the likening of a Demi-God, but you can't afford a roof over your head because all of your time is spent at the gym?

Completing these exercises will arm you with a good idea of what your **Fitness Utopia** will feel and look like. On the next page, write down what you have decided your **Fitness Utopia** will be. Be as specific as you can. Although it should be as clear as possible, the more information, the better! #GetSpecific

MY FITNESS UTOPIA

IS

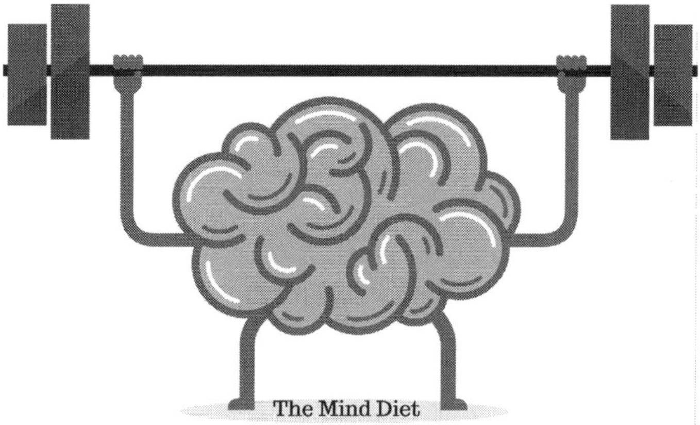

OK. Be honest. How many of you skipped over Step 1a? Did you gloss over it for "a little later?" Perhaps you've found that any genuine attempts to complete this step is quite an unnerving thing to do, and something you rather wouldn't?

This is largely because this step forces you to make a decision about moving your life in a certain direction. A foreseeably uncomfortable direction! A direction plagued with struggle, no Happy Hour, and consistently googling your symptoms after every leg day to self diagnose as many disabilities as you can. A direction (more often than not), you haven't taken before. Or perhaps you have taken, but stopped after only a little time had passed.

Defining what we want in this manner is scary, because we are forging out into the unknown, and …. "OMG where am I, I can't do this, this isn't going to work anyways; it's too much work, I'll do it later… the kids need to be picked up anyway, so let's stop thinking about it and go back to what we were doing before." Sound kind of familiar? (More on self sabotage later.)

Additionally, defining your **Fitness Utopia** forces you to recognize and get honest about where you are currently, (which for many, is an uncomfortable activity.) You may find yourself wondering, "How did I get here? How did I let it go so far?" The answer? You got here by glossing over your **Big What.** Up until this point, you may not have specifically defined your goal, so you could then position yourself in the best place (with the best chance) of achieving and sustaining it.

IF YOU'RE WAITING FOR A SIGN, THIS IS IT.

==> SIGN.

The good thing is, the fat lady hasn't sung yet, friends! If you don't know what your **Big What/Fitness Utopia** is, what are you gonna do about it? You can change the course of your future right now. Go back, put on *'We Are The Champions'* by Queen in the background, muster your most courageous Mufasa face, and decide **specifically** what it is you want to achieve. **Write it down.** Then, write it again and place it somewhere you'll see often. Set a daily morning reminder in your calendar about your goal, and keep it there.

I like to put my first goal down for as soon as I wake up. It's an immediate reminder of the journey I've set out to take as soon as I've opened my eyes.

Defining Your Little What

Congratulations! Now if you have done the exercises correctly, and written down an appropriate **Fitness Utopia**, it will be a lofty, yet specific goal. It can be be assumed that there may be **'little whats'** that need to be achieved first. Your **little whats** funnel like rivers into the ocean, building into the final achievement of your **Big What/Your Fitness Utopia**.

For example, if I would like to lose 20 pounds in time for a trip to Sardinia next summer. I have decided for that to happen, I want to run a marathon. A full marathon is 26.2 miles. Therefore, my **little whats** might be 3 half marathons, and a 5 lbs weight loss each time I run a half marathon. Note the full marathon is also considered a **little what** in this case. My **Fitness Utopia** is reaching my goal of 20 lbs of weight loss for Sardinia June 1st. For reference, I have listed my **little**

whats below:

Deadline	Little What
DATE	HALF MARATHON 5LBS LOST
DATE	HALF MARATHON 5 LBS LOST
DATE	FULL MARATHON 5 LBS LOST
DATE	FITNESS UTOPIA/ SARDINIA TRIP

Here are some more specific examples from past clients that may also help give you some ideas on how to define your **little whats.**

General Fitness Goals	Specific Fitness Goals
"I want to lose weight".	I want to lose 20 Pounds by December which is 8 months away.
"I want to tone up."	I want to put on some lean muscle, like my own version of Kelly Ripa. Although I don't know how much lean muscle, lets start with 2 pounds and then reassess when in one month when I get there!

General Fitness Goals	Specific Fitness Goals
"I want to look good for my wedding"	I want to lose about 8-10 pounds for my wedding 6 months away. I have a picture of what I used to look like 10 years ago, so I want to look like that.
"I want to put on some muscle"	I want to gain 10 pounds of lean muscle by next summer, which is a exactly one year away.
"I want to be healthier"	I want to feel more vitality when I wake up in the morning. I want to lose 5 pounds and put on 5 pounds of lean muscle by the end of the year in 6 months. I want to eat healthy meals everyday & stop smoking and drinking completely by the end of the year.
"I want to be tighter".	I want to put on 5 pounds of lean muscle in two months.

As you can see from these examples, having a specific fitness goal begins to set you up with an action plan of what needs to be done to achieve what you want to achieve. There are specific numbers attached to goals and deadlines that help to then map out your action plan. (More on deadlines later).

Now that you have some examples, it's your turn. Using the same table I have above, define your **little whats** that funnel into achieving your **Big What**, or your **Fitness Utopia**. For simplicity and in order to not get too overwhelmed, **The Mind Diet's** maximum limit for **little whats** at any one time is three. If you have more than that, choose the top three that you believe are the most important to making progress to your **Fitness Utopia**. Rank them in order of achievement, from easiest to hardest.

Step 1b: Define Your Little Whats

DEADLINE	LITTLE WHAT
DATE	
DATE	
DATE	

DATE	FITNESS UTOPIA

Congratulations. Ironically - the biggest and hardest moves we take in fitness and health are not our physical, but our mental steps. By having the courage to complete this very simple yet very difficult task, you are already on your way to being a healthier, happier YOU!

The Lesson

Decide what you want, dammit. #TurnUpforWhat

Chapter 2

But Why, Though?

To invent your own life's meaning is not easy, but it's still allowed, and I think you'll be happier for the trouble.
- Bill Watterson

Very soon after we learn our first words as kids, we start to ask why. If you don't believe me, go and hang out with a 5 year old for the afternoon. They question *everything,* and demand to have meaning as to **why** things are the way they are at every moment.

Through their innocent comprehension, if they are satisfied with the answers given to their questions, and they understand the meaning of why they need to do something (or why they need to behave in a certain way), then everything they do is executed with vitality, obedience and happiness. But if a 5 year old is not given a good enough reason (or worse, no reason at all) to do something, yet is still made to do it - they won't do so without putting up a fight.

As we age, however, something strange happens. We forget just how important our **why** is. We started to ask **why** too much when we were 5 years old, and perhaps eventually, we got into trouble for it. We may have learned a few years later that it was rude to ask why too many times, and ask too many questions.

And now here we are, going through life, doing things, but many of us forget to ask ourselves why we might be doing them. Have you ever found yourself going through the motions, lost in the day to day grind, and just like Kevin Spacey in the film *American Beauty,* you find yourself waking up one day wondering how you got so… "sedated?" More often than not, your **why** has been lost.

Alternatively, you may have a **why,** but this **why** isn't strong enough to hold you accountable to your health and fitness goals when the going gets tough. Your **why** gets conveniently thrown out of the window for an office donut run, or when a boozy Friday night opportunity presents itself: which happens to be: EVERY FRIDAY.

In the area of fitness and health, it is absolutely paramount that you **establish your what and why as early on as possible.** Because (and I am absolutely speaking from experience here), the shit will hit the fan the majority of the time. I can't tell you how many times I've begun working with new eager beaver clients, who are ready and motivated to transform; only to have their plans derailed after a week or two.

When embarking on a fitness journey, the first couple of weeks are a breeze for nearly everyone. Reality check! This doesn't last. At this point, we are are running on pure impulse and adrenaline while the old unhealthy habits still ring true underneath. For sustainable change to occur, deeper work needs to be executed on uprooting old toxic habits hidden in the subconscious, and replacing them with habits conducive to your **Fitness Utopia**. (More on habits in Chapter 7.)

Generally speaking, after two weeks or so of embarking on a fitness overhaul, things start to fall apart from the very foundation. Money troubles, work drama, breakups, going away parties, birthdays, holidays, a sore back, a root canal, a sick child, or the dog eating your healthy meal so you had to eat a burger and fries instead. The list goes on and on, but you get my drift. Something will ALWAYS happen to throw your perfectly planned path to your **Fitness Utopia** off course. Perhaps even off road. Because you driven it off a bridge. And now your car is 3/4 submerged in water. And you can't swim.

The Deal

But luckily, this is life friends. It was never meant to be perfect! And it's never about what happens to you (or around you) that matters anyway. It's what you do **about** what happens to you that does!

So what do you do? You **create your why**. Your **why** will need to be fierce enough to trump all of these mini crisis situations as they occur. Call it Murphy's Law, your Higher

Power testing you, or the Universe having a laugh at your expense. Choosing to make changes in your health is going to rock your world as you know it. You're going to come up against a lot of strong resistance from your existing mindset and environment that would love keep things just as they are. Mediocrity is comfortable. Mediocrity is predictable. You might be fed up with your health right now, but at least it's predictable. It's comfortable. You know what you're gonna get. Sound familiar?

Additionally, change makes people nervous and transformations are messy, and completely un-glamourous. You are changing the status quo and forging out into unchartered waters. Everyone around you will now need to adjust to the new and improved you. By nature, humans are resistant to change, so any expeditions out into the great unknown are going to be met with doubts, fears and criticisms from many around you (as well as from your own inner hater). Sadly (and I am talking from firsthand experience here), you will be unsupported in your endeavors before you are supported. Part of ***The Mind Diet*** is finding individuals that are supportive of your health and journey to greatness. (More on this in Chapter 11, 'A Cheerful Space'.) They are definitely out there, you just need to create the conditions in your own life for that to occur.

So this is *why*, you should have a **why!**

Take another look at the table below of the specific fitness goals that were in Chapter 1. Here, I have added in some examples of what a person's **why** could be.

General Fitness Goals	Specific Fitness Goals
"I want to lose weight".	I want to lose 20 Pounds by December which is 8 months away. I wont give up for my brother, who passed away last year. He would want me to be happy and healthy. This journey is dedicated to him.

General Fitness Goals	Specific Fitness Goals
"I want to tone up."	I want to put on some lean muscle, like my own version of Kelly Ripa. Although I don't know how much lean muscle, lets start with 2 pounds and then reassess when in one month when I get there! I won't give up because I booked a holiday with my best friend and we have made a promise to each other. We are going to get fit together and be the fittest we have ever been on this trip!
"I want to look good for my wedding"	I want to lose about 8-10 pounds for my wedding 6 months away. I have a picture of what I used to look like 10 years ago, so I want to look like that. I wont give up for my wedding and for my husband. I keep imagining what his face will look like when I have lost the weight, feel my best and I get to spend the rest of my life with my soulmate as the best version of myself. It is the best way to enter into my marriage!

General Fitness Goals	Specific Fitness Goals
"I want to put on some muscle"	I want to gain 10 pounds of lean muscle by next summer, which is a exactly one year away. I wont give up because I got bullied in school. I want to do this so then I can go and be a speaker at schools for other boys that might be getting bullied and hope it will inspire them to never give up.
"I want to be healthier"	I want to feel more vitality when I wake up in the morning. I want to lose 5 pounds and put on 5 pounds of lean muscle by the end of the year in 6 months. I want to eat healthy meals everyday & stop smoking and drinking completely by the end of the year. I wont give up because my Doctor has said my cholesterol is incredibly high. I want to be able to play with my kids and be active with them. I do this for them.

General Fitness Goals	Specific Fitness Goals
"I want to be tighter".	I want to put on 5 pounds of lean muscle in two months. I wont give up for my younger self because I used to have an eating disorder. This is my gift to her that being strong and healthy is better than starving yourself. I wont give up either because of other girls that I could help along the way.

Notice how much more effective our Specific fitness goals sound by adding in a **why**? Consider it the kind of premium race fuel you need to ensure the smoothest ride possible to your **Fitness Utopia**. Have you found yourself continually slipping on your health, exercise and nutrition, or starting, but giving up after only a short time has passed? My hunch is that your **why** has not been defined with the detail necessary to make the right decisions when temptation comes around.

Without your **why** specifically defined, you may soon find yourself slipping into your old habits that invoke no change. If you're completely honest with yourself, these are the exact habits that have gotten you to where you are today. To make things a little more complicated, many of these subpar habits are premeditated by the subconscious mind. Because of this, we are unaware that they are even there and that they can be changed.

"So how do I fix thinking about things I don't even know that I think about?" I hear you cry. Define your **what** and **why.** A strong **why** at the forefront of your mind will help you recognize and take a good look at the habits and patterns in your life that have shaped your reality. Paired with a specific and clear **Fitness Utopia** and supporting **little what** will have you looking to make different choices. Choices that are more in line with your fitness goals. Like any new habit, this starts by constant, conscious effort. But with time, consistency and a little bit of good old faith, you'll find your new habits start to stick in that subconscious and voila! A new, healthy habit (in line with your **whats**) have been formed.

Cultivate optimism by committing yourself to a cause, a plan or a value system. You'll feel that you are growing in a meaningful

direction which will help you rise above day-to-day setbacks.
— Dr. Robert Conroy

I think we can agree that there are many different values or causes that can drive an individual to succeed. Your own individual reason *"why"* is not as important as simply having a strong **why** in the first place.

So with that being said: What drives you? Do you know why you do the things you do?

I've always liked this picture of Blake Griffin. He has chosen his family as his **why.** I will argue that nearly all professional athletes are at the level they are at because they have a clear and strongly defined **why**. Their **why** is strong enough to call them to action, get them through grueling training sessions, injuries, stresses of sport, struggles, losses and battles with their own inner critic.

If only The New Years resolution gym goers had a compelling **why** chosen at the forefront of their minds when they entered the gym January 1, many would have continued well past February and beyond. Statistics show the average time it takes for humans to fall off on their New Years Resolution goals is between two and a half, to just under three weeks. It never matters what the type of training, intensity, what the cardio to weights split is, or what their nutrition is like. We fall off. And why? One of the main reasons is their **why** was either non existent, or not strong enough to push them past the growing pains of changing their habits to foster lasting change.

So, just as every weight should have a mate in the gym, your **Fitness Utopia** should have a supporting **big why.** Additionally, every **little what** you have created should also be accompanied with a supporting **little why**. These **little whys** may or may not be the same as your **big why.**

The Mind Diet works best when choosing a **little why** that has the biggest chance of propelling you into action. Although our **Big Why** can be the overall reason why we walk in our purpose through life, (and is the umbrella reason for doing anything), your **little whys** could be more goal orientated or can be a **why** that progresses you further along your path to your **Big What/Fitness Utopia.**

The Deal on Your Big Why

Newsflash: It ain't about you.

Although your **Big Why** is an individual thing, I have found that your **Big Why** will invariably be more successful if it isn't about you. I get it, we all want to get fit and healthy so we can rock a bikini at the beach, or be known in all of the cosmos as the sexiest man of all time. But choosing something other than yourself will hold you accountable to something other than you, and/or ideally, greater than you.

So who gets you going? Who adds rhyme to your reason, and reason to your rhyme? Who would you fight to the death to protect? Perhaps your **Big W** is about God. Maybe it's about your family, husband, wife or kids. Your **Big Why** will need to be something strong enough to call you to action through struggle, being unmotivated and tired or even wanting to completely give up.

> **You will find the meaning in life only if you create it. It is not lying there somewhere behind the bushes, so you can go and you search a little bit and find it. It is not there like a rock that you will find. It is a poetry to be composed, it is a song to be sung, it is a dance to be danced.**
>
> **- Osho**

A Why of Spite

OK. As I have mentioned before, **Big Why** and **little whys** are yours to choose, and yours alone. No one knows you better than you. **The Mind Diet** is largely about self exploration and figuring out your own personal traits and triggers. You can then harness these triggers to work in line with your health goals, and the journey to your best self. There are no wrong answers to anything; only individual discoveries and lessons on your path to greatness.

So perhaps if you've started mapping out your **Big/little whys,** you have allocated one of your **whys** to be to get back at someone. Your **why** is what I like to call "a **why** of spite." For example, maybe you went through a horrible breakup where someone dumped you. Fresh out of tears, you are ready to take revenge. You have decided your **Fitness Utopia** is to completely transform your body to Victoria Secret Model status: Adriana Lima style. Being straight out of the breakup, your **Big Why** is to make your ex regret dumping you for the rest of his life, and you can't wait to see the look on his face in six months time when you post your pictures of your holiday in Barbados with your new boyfriend who just so happens to be Shemar Moore or Liam Hemsworth. (Or both.) They are both on holiday with you, and you have two boyfriends. And if anyone was ever to have the audacity to ask why you have two boyfriends, you will say they are wrong for saying that, because Orlando Bloom is waiting for you back at home. So, in actual fact, you have three boyfriends. Your ex is going to be so mad! Yay!

Now, believe me, I get it. Spite can be great for lighting a fire under our butts, particularly if we are fresh from the event that is causing the spite (or upset) within us in the first place. I've had many successful transformations occur in front of me because the person was going through a divorce, or a tragedy of some kind. This is because their **what** and **why** is strong. In the case of a breakup or tragedy, the person's **why** is chosen for them by default.

If you have chosen a **why** of spite however, it's been my experience that these results never last. This is because time usually dilutes the potency of that **why**. Psychologists say (and by psychologists I mean Google), the average time to get over a divorce or breakup is approximately 3 months. And then what? Once you're fresh outta spite, what's gonna wake you up in the morning? Are you going to be breaking up with one of your three boyfriends so your spite can keep bearing fruit?

In order to keep that **why** of spite fresh to propel you into action, and in order for it to keep doing what it is supposed to do, you will consciously need to keep your body in a state of spite, long after the spite probably would've left you in any normal circumstance. I will discuss more about creating habits in Chapter 7, but you don't need to be a rocket scientist to see how destructive this is. When you're trying to rise into your best self, choosing a **why** of spite puts your body at a frequency that is not conducive to optimal health. I doubt anyone can maintain a peak level of health and happiness while that type of energy hangs around like a bad smell.

Maybe you are fresh out of a relationship, or you are trying to get back at someone. It's natural to feel these things and go through the process, and perhaps the spite **why** you have chosen is honestly very effective for you at the moment. So honor this place, and use it to fuel your growth and transformation, but recognize that **The Mind Diet** encourages you to always look for a way to raise your cheerful vibes and know that one day, you will need to let this spite and this toxic **why** go in order to step into your true greatness, and best version of you. There is no way around it!

Step 2a/2b:
Define Your Little and Big Why

At the end of the day, there is no meaning to life unless if we create one. This rings true for your fitness goals too. On the following page, list your **Big Why** and place it somewhere you see it everyday. Attach appropriate **little whys** to each **little what.** Then set a reminder in your calendar for when your alarm goes off, and have these reminders repeat themselves at various times during the day.

The aim is that every day when you wake up and your reminder goes off, you are immediately reminded of your **what** and **why.** Currently, my reminders have been set at the following times. Follow mine along, or choose your own times that you know you'll be able to see it easily when it goes off.

I NEVER GIVE UP

FOR

6am

11.30am

5pm

9pm

Warning: Following this, you may find your workouts possess an energy and vitality that would put your 5 year old self to shame. Train your mind to associate your health and fitness with never giving up. Then use your **why** to motivate your actions that get you closer to your **little whats**, that lead into to arriving at your **Fitness Utopia.** It's so simple, but it works!

The Lesson

Be your annoying 5 year old self and always remember to ask **why!**

Chapter 3

The Big D (Deadline)

A goal without a deadline is just a dream.
- Gail Vaz-Oxlade

I am an Australian expat living in Los Angeles. Every three years or so, I have had to lodge a petition with the US government that proves my visa status is still applicable for me. It's an arduous process of collecting documentation from companies and individuals that I have worked with, future contracts of work, character references, and a copy of all of the completed work I have done over the years. The document is in excess of 800 pages and needs to be neatly collated and easily referenced for approval.

How I always predict this process will go:

I know my expiration date three years in advance. Therefore, I have three years to continually update and gather the necessary documents, so it can be lodged easily for approval with time to spare. I start a color-coded and alphabetically indexed file that is neatly labelled with a black felt pen that doesn't smudge. Hell, you can even write upside down with this felt pen. As each job or contract is completed, I collate the paperwork neatly, and gather professional references appropriately on their official company letterhead with signatures.

How the process actually goes down:

My visa is expiring tomorrow. I have no flight out of the US, but I definitely need one. I need to find the contracts from … what was that job? Oh and I gotta get that reference from so and so … *oh no,* but they're away till next week and where the devil did I put my press articles, ahh my ink just ran out in my printer, who will look after my cat while I wait for my visa to process and where the hell am I going OMG!! I need a flight somewhere but they are so expensive & I have no clue where my passport is — #MAYDAY #Houston #MyWalkieTalkieIsDead !!!

Ahem.

Now, I am not saying that all of you are like me. But I'm just gonna assume that most of you are. We're humans, and for whatever reason, we are prone to being lazy. Come on, let's just cut the crap, call a spade a spade, and get honest with ourselves. How often do you actually do something when there is no urgency to do so? Less often than you care to admit, right? Don't worry, I'm guilty of this too! We've got so many things in the, 'I'll get to it later pile', when there has been ample opportunity and time to have these things completed; often years beforehand. Sadly, (but all too often) our fitness and health is usually in this '*someday pile*', along with your cruise to Alaska, your sky diving adventure and your volunteer work at the kitten shelter because you always say it's very important for you to give back. Sound familiar?

What would you do differently if someone told you that you were dying?
Well you are. We all are.

Sometimes, our health slides so far south that you're red flagged by the Health Gods, and life creates a deadline for you. Change or you will expire soon! Impeding disease, sickness, or injuries that seriously threaten your quality of life. It's a shame we are naturally wired to wait until the last minute to respond to our wake up call and act. Knowing this however, how can we best proceed?

Step 3: Create A Deadline

So, you know **what** you want. You know **why** you want it. Do you know **when?**

You can have game changing fitness goals and the best reasons for doing them. But unless you commit to a deadline in real time, you run the risk of leaving it in the '*someday pile*'... well, for someday. And although I have checked, I am yet to see a day called Someday appear on a calendar.

This is your life, folks! It's up to you only to create the urgency for yourself. Trust me, no one will want it for you more than you. Similar to Step 1 and Step 2 of **The Mind Diet**, it doesn't matter specifically **when,** as long as there is a **when** to work with. Scheduling your **when** is another crucial step in your plan. It's like you're putting your car into drive and your foot is on the gas pedal. The wheels are moving, and you will soon begin to map out your path of actions to get there.

Either you run the day or the day runs you.
- Jim Rohn

Let's take another look at the common fitness goals from Chapter 1. Knowing Steps 1-3, we can now see how effective the specific fitness goals are in setting yourself up for success below.

General Fitness Goals	Specific Fitness Goals
"I want to lose weight".	I want to lose 20 Pounds by December which is 8 months away. I refuse to give up for my brother, who passed away last year. He would want me to be happy and healthy. This journey is dedicated to him.
"I want to tone up."	I want to put on some lean muscle, like my own version of Kelly Ripa. Although I don't know how much lean muscle, lets start with 2 pounds and then reassess when in one month when I get there! I won't give up because I booked a holiday with my best friend in 4 months and we have made a promise to each other. We are going to get fit together and be the fittest we have ever been on this trip!

General Fitness Goals	Specific Fitness Goals
"I want to look good for my wedding"	I want to lose about 8-10 pounds for my wedding 6 months away. I have a picture of what I used to look like 10 years ago, so I want to look like that. I won't give up on my wedding for my husband. I keep imagining what his face will look like when I have lost the weight, feel my best and I get to spend the rest of my life with my soulmate as the best version of myself. It is the best way to enter into my marriage!
"I want to put on some muscle"	I want to gain 10 pounds of lean muscle by next summer, which is a exactly one year away. I won't give up because I got bullied in school. I want to do this so I can be a speaker at schools for other boys that might be getting bullied, in the hope it will inspire them to never give up.

General Fitness Goals	Specific Fitness Goals
“I want to be healthier”	I want to feel more vitality when I wake up in the morning. I want to lose 5 pounds and put on 5 pounds of lean muscle by the end of the year in 6 months. I want to eat healthy meals everyday & stop smoking and drinking completely by the end of the year. I won’t give up because my Doctor has said my cholesterol is incredibly high. I want to be able to play with my kids and be active with them. I do this for them.
“I want to be tighter”.	I want to put on 5 pounds of lean muscle in two months. I won't give up on my younger self, who had an eating disorder. My gift to her, and to the many other girls out there with the same problem, will be showing them that being strong and healthy is better than starving yourself.

Successfully defining fitness goals so you have the best chance of success consist of specifically **what** you want to achieve,

when you want to achieve it by and **why** you are committing to this change. Together your **what, why,** and **when** makes up what **The Mind Diet** refers to as the **3W.** Note that your **whens** are simply dates that you have set up in your calendar to correspond with the supporting **little whats, little whys** and your **Fitness Utopia.**

Take Responsibility For The Big D

It is up to you to take responsibility of your fitness goals, and create your own **whens.** Whether it is for a holiday you've booked in three months, a half marathon you signed up for next January, your wedding in one year, or an arbitrary date like January 18th: *choose your when date.* After this, **you do not deviate** from this date*.

**very important*

I have always found that setting your **when,** then immediately solidifying these commitments is a winning action you can take to begin the forward motion of change and progress in your health and life. Some great examples include purchasing tickets, hotels, committing to a friend about your goal event, and/or setting multiple daily reminders in your calendar of your **what** and your **why.**

When is **The Big D** for you? Write yours down on the following page.

THE BIG D

T MINUS

Remember, as we touched on in Chapter 2, once these small actions are taken and the energy of change is activated, it is alarming, yet all too predictable how life will try and pull you off course, back into the equilibrium of your past habits of half results and fitness mediocrity. Committing to **when** is a great way to raise the stakes, maintain the urgency and keep you on the most efficient track to your **Fitness Utopia.**

Little D (Deadlines) Stop

Great things are done by a series of small things brought together.
- Vincent Van Gogh

You will find that if the first three steps of **The Mind Diet** are executed correctly, you can set some **'little d'** stops to serve as necessary benchmarks that work as a sequential lead up to the achievement of each **little what,** and of course **Big D** finale. Obviously **little d** stops are positioned on a case-by-case situation. Let's start with one of the examples:

General Fitness Goals	Specific Fitness Goals
"I want to look good for my wedding"	I want to lose about 8-10 pounds for my wedding 2 months away. I have a picture of what I used to look like 10 years ago, so I want to look like that. I won't give up on my wedding for my husband. I keep imagining what his face will look like when I have lost the weight, feel my best and I get to spend the rest of my life with my soulmate as the best version of myself. It is the best way to enter into my marriage!

For the purposes of my own amusement only, we can call this client Becky. Becky has come so far already. She has gotten specific and has defined what "look good for my wedding" really means to her. Working with many clients over the years, I can tell you first hand that 'looking cute and fit' is highly subjective to the individual. Beauty is in the eye of the beholder, as they say! All definitions are 100% valid, however it is important for both of us to have a clear idea of **what,**

when and why so we can get Becky to where she wants to go with no confusion, and in the quickest manner possible.

BECKY MONTH 1

	WEEK 1	WEEK 2	WEEK3	WEEK 4
SUN	1 VISUALIZATION & PLANNING FOR THE WEEK	8 VISUALIZA TION & PLANNING FOR THE WEEK	15 VISUALIZATION & PLANNING FOR THE WEEK	22 VISUALIZATION & PLANNING FOR THE WEEK
MON	2 *LITTLE D STOP 1-2LBS	9 *LITTLE D STOP 1-2LBS	16 *LITTLE D STOP 1-2LBS	23 *LITTLE D STOP 1-2LBS
TUES	3	10	17	24
WED	4 BALLOONS MUSCLE UP	11 BALLOONS MUSCLE UP	18 BALLOONS MUSCLE UP	25 BALLOONS MUSCLE UP
THURS	5 PAY IT FORWARD MUSCLE UP	12 PAY IT FORWARD MUSCLE UP	19 PAY IT FORWARD MUSCLE UP	26 PAY IT FORWARD MUSCLE UP
FRI	6	13	20	27
SAT	7 *LITTLE D STOP PERSONAL WEIGH IN & CHEAT MEAL	14 *LITTLE D STOP PERSONAL WEIGH IN & CHEAT MEAL	21 *LITTLE D STOP PERSONAL WEIGH IN & CHEAT MEAL	28 *LITTLE D STOP PERSONAL WEIGH IN & CHEAT MEAL *LITTLE D STOP TOTAL MONTH LOSS 4-5 LBS

BECKY MONTH 2

	WEEK 1	WEEK 2	WEEK 3	WEEK 4
SUN	1. VISUALIZATION & PLANNING FOR THE WEEK	8 VISUALIZATION & PLANNING FOR THE WEEK	15 VISUALIZATION & PLANNING FOR THE WEEK	22 VISUALIZATION & PLANNING FOR THE WEEK
MON	2 *LITTLE D STOP LOSS 4-5 LBS REWARD SPA TREAT	9	16	23
TUES	3	10	17	24
WED	4 BALLOONS MUSCLE UP	11 BALLOONS MUSCLE UP	18 BALLOONS MUSCLE UP	25 BALLOONS MUSCLE UP
THURS	5 PAY IT FORWARD MUSCLE UP	12 PAY IT FORWARD MUSCLE UP	19 PAY IT FORWARD MUSCLE UP	26 PAY IT FORWARD MUSCLE UP
FRI	6	13	20	27
SAT	7 *LITTLE D STOP PERSONAL WEIGH IN & CHEAT MEAL	14 *LITTLE D STOP PERSONAL WEIGH IN & CHEAT MEAL	21 *LITTLE D STOP PERSONAL WEIGH IN & CHEAT MEAL	28 *LITTLE D STOP PERSONAL WEIGH IN & CHEAT MEAL

Check out Becky's calendar on the previous page. Along with the summary below, you can use this as an example to get started on your own calendar!

Based on Becky's current goals, she is looking at a 1-2 pound loss in weight per week, which in fitness professional land is within the standard guidelines of healthy weight-loss. Perfect! Knowing this, **little d** stops can now be set up using the following suggestions:

1. Becky would like to do the Balloon Drop (page 23) exercise in letting go of toxicity. She has scheduled it on every Sunday, in order to prepare her for the week ahead. She has a list of things in mind she has identified as toxic habits in her life that she will tackle and amend as the time progresses.

2. Every Monday is a scheduled **little d** stop. She needs to be 2 pounds less than the week before. 1 pound would be OK at the start, and we could reassess after a few weeks to see how far we had to go.

3. At the end of Month 1, there is also another **little d** stop.

Ideally, she would be 5lbs down, however as her range is 8-10 pounds, we would be happy with a 4lbs loss in weight. If she is successful in meeting this deadline, she is allowed to take her luxurious appointment at the spa she has booked as a reward for staying on track.

4. We have worked together to set up a nutrition program focusing on her weight-loss. Becky has chosen her cheat meal as Saturday night. She has set this up as another a **little d** stop. She will do a weigh-in herself, and if she is not at the forecasted target, she will choose to skip her cheat meal this week and give herself the opportunity for another workout session on Sunday.

5. Every morning, there is a **little d** stop set up for Becky to spend 5-10 minutes looking at her Vision Board and remembering her **Big What/Fitness Utopia** and **Big Why**. She loves to visualize her perfect wedding day walking down the aisle and imagining the details of what that is about! In her vision, she has great hair, she is 10 pounds down, and she fits perfectly into her wedding dress. She feels no shame when her (now) husband picks her up and swings her over the threshold, something she

would have been so uncomfortable with before. This makes her so happy knowing she feels good in her skin. She is also ready for her honeymoon straight after in the Bahamas, where she plans on living in a bikini that she has bought already. It is hanging next to her vision board and it is a size smaller than what she usually wears currently.

Clearly, how particular you get is largely individual, but I would advise that without getting too robotic about it, the more specific **little d** stops you have scheduled, the better equipped you will be in moving in the right direction and not succumbing to the storms of change. **The Mind Diet** will touch further on the importance of rewards a little later on, but I have found that rewarding yourself for your progress by scheduling small rewards in line with your **little d** stops are very effective actions you can do to create and maintain momentum. Plus, you feel good about yourself, add an extra layer of accountability, enjoyment and positive reinforcement. Simply put: it's fun as hell to treat yourself! So why not create the conditions where you can do so without guilt, while still moving towards your health and fitness goals at the same time? #BeckyYouGotThis

The Lesson

We all have the power to be cruising into **The Big D** with the top down and the wind in our hair, we simply need to plan it out and create the space and ideal conditions for the magic to happen! #Easy

Chapter 4

Jump!

To begin, begin.
- William Wordsworth

When I was in high school in Australia, we were required to go away on a school camp once a year. This would usually be somewhere in the depths of the bush. We would camp in tents and hike for miles, all while fighting off leeches or other strange Australian creepy crawlers. As part of the curriculum, we were required to complete various group and team activities: the primary aim being to help us grow into well rounded individuals that could share and play well with others in a socially acceptable manner. So basically, an effort to make sure we were aware that jail was a place that we weren't allowed to end up at, and that it was preferable for us to behave in a manner that was acceptable for others around us at all times.

One year there was a very important exercise that still sticks with me till this day. At the time, I didn't understand the magnitude of this activity and how it would shape the fabric of my entire life. As an adult now, I think of it whenever I am about to make a big decision.

The activity was this: we were required to put on some rock climbing attire and equipment and climb up a cliff to a mountain top. We were attached to a safety pulley system to the camp leader down on the ground, perhaps some 20 meters below. The challenge was to jump off the cliff, extend our arms out, and catch a metal beam that was hanging horizontally past the cliff's edge. The beam could not be reached unless if you got a running start from the top of the cliff and quite literally, hurled yourself off. This was a real time creation of "Cirque De Soleil Outback Australia Edition" for high-school amateurs.

Even if you are afraid of heights like me, it's always an unnerving feeling, standing at the edge of a cliff, looking down below. Wondering if this was how it was all going to end. I was 16 at the time, full of nervous energy with butterflies in my stomach. The rest of my camp group looked up at me from down below with our camp leader. This was high-school, so doing something embarrassing right now would be school suicide. Frantic thoughts of accidentally wetting my pants and falling to my death (while everyone watched and laughed) filled my thoughts.

Standing at the edge with my legs shaking, I looked down at the camp leader. He asked me to talk to him (and if I wanted to), to vocalize what was going through my head. I called out that I was too high up, and I didn't like heights. He replied, "Then don't look down!"

I forced my eye line away from the camp leader and the smirks of my camp group below. I looked straight ahead at the metal beam hanging out there in the middle of the abyss.

It was in that moment, as I focused on the beam, that suddenly my mind went eerily quiet. From that day, a new pattern in my life was born.

"I'm going to jump." I called out to him.

Now, I'd be lying if I didn't tell you there was a micro moment after my launch from the ground where a sense of extreme panic overcame me. That a horrible mistake had been made and I was now experiencing my final moments here on Earth. However, as quickly as the panic had set in, it had disappeared. On cue, my hands extended out and I grabbed the metal beam. Shaking and hanging there in the middle of the air, I had made it. I was still alive. Great success!

> **You can't be that kid standing at the top of the waterslide, overthinking it. You have to go down the chute.**
> **– Tina Fey**

Even though that was longer ago than I care to admit, when I am faced with making an uncomfortable decision that will give me the choice of being a step closer to my **what,** I like to

imagine myself back on that cliff, standing on the edge with my legs shaking and butterflies in my stomach.
I know I need to jump. Eventually I do. Because ever since that day, that's what I decided that I would always do.

So hypothetically, maybe you are standing out on the cliff with me. You've created the perfect path to your dream body, and your dream health. You have your motivational quotes, your vision board is on Pinterest, and your workout routine is mapped out. You've set the conditions up to succeed. You're prepared to knock out any obstacles that may occur with your **why** at the forefront of your mind. Now, all there is left to do is **jump.** To begin!

But the sad thing is, most people will not jump. Why?

The F Word

If you're afraid of heights like I am, you might be thinking the F word is something you'll be yelling down to the camp leader, or at the very least, yelling at him inside your head (as well as every other curse word under the sun.) I'm not talking about that F word though.

The F word I'm referring to is a lot more toxic than that. It's the cause of all human feet never leaving the ground. The root of all inaction. The reason a person's potential is never fully realized. It freezes progression, understanding and growth. It has the power to diffuse compassion. It can also stop love **dead in its tracks.**

fear.

It's written in small font and it doesn't even deserve a capital letter, Because once you see it for what it really is, then **you can make the choice** to let it have no power over you. When you succumb to your fearful actions (or shall I say fearful inactions), nothing will change in your health and fitness. You may find small changes begin to occur, then all of a sudden you are back to where you started. Sound familiar?

Out there on the cliff, fear can come in many shapes and forms, including:

Overthinking

Welcome to analysis paralysis. I'll admit I am the Queen of this. I love nothing more than to straddle each leg over the fence of indecision, and ride that bitch like a professional cowgirl. The only thing is, the fence doesn't move. Neither do I. And while I'm here weighing my pros and cons out, no decisions are made. When nothing gets decided: you guessed it! **Nothing gets done, and nothing is changed.**

So out there on the almighty cliff, when the stakes are high it can seem like a much better option to not jump **yet.** Overthinking kicks into high gear. Now that you think about it, maybe it would be better not to start this week, because you have a staff work party coming up, and it's guaranteed to be a boozy lunch. And hmm, maybe your fitness goals are a little too lofty for your current workload and the date you have set for **The Big D**. Maybe you should read another book about nutrition and training. You know, just to make sure you are set up for the right diet and supplement plan for your goal. Now that you think about it, maybe you should hire a new trainer that's more in line with your fitness goals. Oh shoot! You need new workout shoes because your current shoes have a hole in them. And you need new workout clothes too, so you should go shopping first…blah, blah, blah < insert overthinking, psychotic, procrastinating, anxiety driven, and ultimately unproductive thoughts here. >

Fear of Failure

Imagine being afraid of something that hasn't even happened yet, and may never, ever, happen. But you are so afraid of it, that you do nothing about it. This is fear of failure.

The next chapter of this book is dedicated to exercises you can add into your own program to ensure you are keeping the fear of failure monsters at bay. I have dealt with this issue a lot in my life, so I know first-hand how debilitating it can be! To foster lasting change in your health, and to become a game changer in anything you want to do in life, you will need to face your fear of failure and overcome it. There is no way around it!

A Weak Why

We covered how important our **why** is in **The Mind Diet** in Chapter 2. But it's worth mentioning again here. A strong and appropriate **why** would be just the reason to **jump.** It would be strong enough to force us to act in a manner that would move us closer to our fitness goals every day. But as we know, most people don't jump because they have chosen a weak **why**. And the main reason that weak **why/s** are chosen is due to fear.

We are afraid of what a strong **why** would have the capacity to do. Choosing a strong **why** would mean our feet would leave the ground and essentially the safety of everything we know. And back here on the ground, even though it is unsettling, at least you know what you're getting. Ring a bell?

Self Sabotage

There is self help mumbo jumbo out there that states that we accept a love we believe we deserve, and a life we believe we deserve. It's also fair to say we accept a body we believe we deserve. Although I will delve deeper into the topic of self worth later on, it's worth mentioning now that out there on the cliff, it's common to sabotage our **jump** for our fitness goals because we don't believe we deserve the health, or the body that we are asking for. Maybe that seems unbelievable to you. "Why wouldn't I want the chiseled body of Zac Efron, Edwina?", you might ask. Or, "Of course I would allow my spirit to embody a clone of Jillian Michaels physique if I was given the chance!"

Now hear me out:

I want you to think about an example in your life when an event occurred that you can define as utterly unacceptable for you. An event in which you feel you were unjustly treated. It doesn't need to be fitness and health related. Perhaps your partner cheated on you. Perhaps you were betrayed by a close friend, or a family member. Perhaps someone stole something from you.

Take a moment to reflect on what happened specifically. How did you react in this situation? Did you yell and scream? Did you make a stand and say, enough is enough? Did you take immediate action to move away from the toxic event/person/

thing that happened? Today, are your current actions still embodying damage control, ensuring that this event (or events like this) will not recur in the future because it was unjustly deserved?

So, why is it that our mediocre health is not given the same courtesy? If we can agree that everything we define as completely unacceptable and undeserving is not in our lives, can we **then** agree that you accept your current level of health because you believe you are deserving of it? #ThinkAboutIt

And just to hammer the nail in the coffin, can we agree that if in fact you are aware and unhappy of your health right now, but continue to **not** do the things you know you need to do to make changes, it is fair to say you do not feel **deserving enough of health** to have the changes take place, and have your world transform as you know it?

Top Excuses For Not Taking Care Of Your Health

Listed below are The New York Times top ten reasons why people believe they are not at their ideal level of health and fitness in their lives currently.

1. I have no time. I'm too busy.
2. I'm too old.
3. I don't want to do it alone.
4. It's boring.
5. My kids get in the way.
6. My back hurts.
7. I'm too fat.
8. I'm thin already.
9. I hate the gym.
10. I have arthritis.

Is the main reason you have not achieved the results you would have liked listed above?

Now let's do a quick exercise. I want you to imagine you are standing in front of me. While speaking aloud, tell me why you aren't where you should be in your health and wellness today. Phrase it along the lines of this:

"The reason I do not have the health and fitness I should have is: < then insert your reason here.>".

Now repeat the sentence aloud again, but replace your reason with:

" I do not feel deserving enough of it."

How does speaking this aloud make you feel? What thoughts, feelings and emotions come up? Defensiveness? Sadness? Curiosity?

There are no wrong answers, just individual discoveries. If writing is cathartic for you, take some time now to write about how that sentence makes you feel. If you are okay with sharing, talk about it with a partner or friend. Share with them, or write of the first time you can remember that you didn't feel deserving of something.

In the developed world, subpar health and fitness, obesity levels and healthcare costs are on the rise, and plague the majority population today. Much of being in expensive therapy sessions goes into uncovering the (mostly) subconscious reasons we feel the way we do. From there, we learn to consciously reprogram those old toxic thought patterns, for a healthier, more successful alternative. Alternatives that are in harmony to achieving the **3W's** that you have chosen for your **Mind Diet**. Modern psychotherapy would argue that it is those defining events as children that shape our thoughts and habits. Over time, these thoughts, patterns and habits become engrained as part of our subconscious. They are the foundation from which we function, and the brick and mortar that we build our health, our body and essentially our entire lives on.

The Deal

For goodness sake, this is your life, friend! And it's happening, whether you're ready or not. So it seems you woke up once day and you realize you're 40 lbs heavier. No one on Earth is spared from their own personal setbacks and crisis situations. Annoying health issues, an injury, a sagging tummy line, being cursed by the laziness gods, or whatever tragedy that has happened to you that can account for the current state of your fitness and health. But as I mentioned previously, it's never about what happens to you. It's what you do **after** what happens to you that makes all the difference!

> **You never drown by falling into water. You drown by staying there.**
> **- Edwin Lewis Cole**

I'm not going to lie to you. It's taken time to build these habits; often years. So it will take time to change them. One of the most heartbreaking things I see as a fitness professional is the frustration from clients who are a few weeks into their new program. They have made some great changes, but it's still not fast enough for their liking. So, they give up before the really good changes start to occur. Or, maybe it is too fast for their comfortability, and they self sabotage their progress; due to their mental fitness game not being exercised with the same consistency or intensity as their physical body.

The truth is, I am still seeing changes after ten years of consistent training. You see, rumor has it that the fitness fairies work their magic in secret, and the changes are incremental day to day. And I get it! It can be hard not to be disheartened in this current society of instant gratification. Fitness scams fill our media with false promises of extreme weight loss in unreasonable amounts of time. These scams plague the health and fitness industry today, and do not give an accurate representation of the effort and time needed to get you the results outlined in your **what/s** or the real time required to look like the person you've seen in your personal **Fitness Utopia** mirror.

If you're health isn't at an ideal level currently, the reality is that it took some time to get there. Naturally, it will take some time to lose (or change). It involves a consistent and lasting change in your thoughts, habits and lifestyle. In the meantime, there's no harm in enjoying the journey, having a smile on your face and being kind to yourself. You're doing the best you can! Ask yourself, what can I do **right now** to help move me to my next **little d?** Step up to your mountains edge, take a deep breath then,

JUMP.

Jump, even though deep down, you may not think you deserve it. Jump, because you haven't jumped before. Jump, because you already know what's on the ground, and my thoughts are this: if you really liked what was there, you wouldn't be reading this book.

JUMP!

It will seem uncanny to you how these thoughts simply fade away the moment your feet leave the ground. In time it may feel similar to your favorite activity because I promise you, once you get going, it will become one of your favorite things to do!

Think back to a pastime that you loved so much that time seemed to stand still while you were doing it. For me, snowboarding always comes to mind. There is something so peaceful and present about being in nature, not hearing anything but the sound of your board carving from side to side as you ride down the mountain. It is routine for 6 hours to pass before the thought even comes to me that I have not eaten or had a sip of water. (By the way, I am not recommending this as some kind of new age weight-loss strategy, you crazy cats.) I use this as an example because this is one of the most enjoyable activities on Earth for me. Because I am completely committed to the **act of doing**, my mind is still. So it might be meditation for you. Maybe it's knitting. Get excited, because you're about to enter that zone. Decide to jump, and then in the famous cliche of Nike, #JustDoIt. Jump! One time.

All of your favorite fitness personalities, professional athletes, or any outlier that you admire have all experienced that one defining point where they've had an opportunity to jump and they did. They jumped, even though they had never jumped before. They jumped, despite conditions being less than perfect. They jumped before they were ready.

Now, if you are honest with yourself, you'll see the **same level of opportunities** that exist for those outliers, are the **same levels of opportunities** that are available to you. The same opportunities for greatness. In the game of life, (whether you are aware of it or not), my guess is that you have seen many mountain edges already. You were given the choice to jump, and fly to the beam, or to stay on the ground in the same place. Every outlier has stood on their own personal mountain cliff, and has hurled themselves off the edge without knowing what would happen. It's these continual jumps that define them as the outliers they are today.

Calm Down, Tiger.

Now, if you're about to get into your car and drive to the nearest cliff and hurl yourself off it, please don't. I'll get into big trouble. Recognize that everyone's first **jump** is different. It doesn't need to be a high stakes situation to set the wheels in motion to your **Fitness Utopia.** Perhaps from the outset, your **jump** is a seemingly small action (similar to the jumps I have described in Chapter 3): booking a ticket, telling a trusted friend of your commitment to health, joining the gym, or throwing out all of the junk food in your house. It doesn't matter. Congratulations! **A jump is still a jump!**

> **Just do yourself a favor. Jump. One time.**
> **Jump. Just jump.**
> **- Steve Harvey**

If you're listening to your heart and your intuition, you'll know when you need to make the leap. You'll feel the energy of change in the air, and the change within yourself. You might feel restless, or more frustrated than usual. This is your sign that something needs to change. Meditate on your **what** and

why. Listen for the path to appear, and prepare to launch!

After The First Jump

You may find that after your initial jump, you'll want to become a jumping junkie. Use this energy of forward motion to add more fuel to the fire to make bigger jumps, and build that momentum to change those unhealthy, unconscious health habits that you've held onto for so long. Life will suddenly take on an adventurous tone, and over time you'll find yourself jumping all of the time and not even thinking about it. Congratulations! A new habit has been created. It's fun out on the beam! Do enough of these jumps, and you'll be rolling into **The Big D** with the top down, wondering why you created such a fuss about it in the first place.

My Jumps

In the interests of sharing and solidarity with my fellow mountain cliff jumpers, I'd like to share some of my most notable and life changing jumps with you below:

- Quitting a new full-time job in financial services to work at a gym. This is after three years of arduous study, and receiving an Economics and Business degree at one of the top universities in Australia.
- Leaving Australia and everything I'd ever known behind to move to NYC on my own.
- Leaving NYC on a whim, and flying to Vancouver, Canada where I lived for three years.
- Leaving Canada to move to Los Angeles with no working visa, knowing one person that I'd met two weeks previously, and having no clue how I was going to get my legal residency.
- Writing this book and sharing **The Mind Diet** with the world.
- Stepping onstage and doing my first fitness competition.
- Falling in love.
- Shaving my head.
- Walking away from negativity and disrespect at all costs, even though in many cases it was all I knew.
- Literally jumping into opportunities that feel joyful without guilt.

- Loving money and what it can do for me without shame.

Step 4: JUMP!

Now it's your turn to share. Start a list of your own jumps using the table at the end of this chapter. Refer back to this list often! When I'm standing on my own mountain's edge faced with making a decision, I always find it helps to refer back to my past jumps. It gives me an extra push to take that leap. In the day-to-day grind, (and especially if you have big goals planned), it can be easy to forget what you have accomplished.

Referring back to this list is a great way to track your **jumps** and doubles as a useful motivational tool. Whenever I'm contemplating a **jump** and I read my list, it always gives me that confidence I need to **jump** again. It reminds me of my first time on the cliff when I decided to **jump.** I've landed OK all of those times before… and I'm gonna be just fine this time too!

Now - immediately choose a task you've written that can be achieved the fastest. Make the conscious choice to jump. Then jump and go and do it.

Welcome to the party on the beam!

The Lesson

Jump! #JustDoIt

JUMPS

Chapter 5

Mental Muscle Ups

Have you ever tried to do a muscle up? Were you successful in doing so? One of the most used movements in CrossFit and Calisthenics, the muscle up is a pull-up to a dip in one smooth transition. It's a specific skill that involves isolating certain muscles while moving others. It also requires developing your ability to hold your own bodyweight (as you transition through the movement), from the bottom of the bar to the top.

The Mind Diet can be thought of as a toolbox. Within this book, you'll find many tools to use in the toolbox that you can take out and schedule for use. They are called **Mental Moves.**

They exist to keep you motivated to act in line with your **3W** and to always be moving you towards your **Fitness Utopia.**

Within the **Mental Moves** are what I like to call mental muscle ups. It's based on the pretense that though your brain is technically an organ, it behaves just like a muscle. Similar to training your glutes or your chesticles for a certain goal, through practicing certain movements or patterns, you can also *train your mind* to improve cognitive functions, and **create a habit** for it to behave (first) consciously, (then) subconsciously in a certain pattern to achieve a certain result. Have you ever met that person that's always happy all of the time? Well, they've trained their mind to think like that!

Similar to a normal muscle up, a mental muscle up needs to be practiced and used often, or you'll lose the ability to execute it smoothly, (and eventually lose the ability to execute it altogether.) It's a cold world, and a "you snooze, you lose" mentality exists for both a normal muscle up, and all of the mental muscle ups in **The Mind Diet**. This is because the human body is a very adaptable entity, and looks to relocate energy (and resources), when it stops being used in any particular manner.

When effectively performed, deploying mental muscle ups can be likened to adding a fuel injection into a race car. These muscle ups can be responsible for the difference between you standing on your mountain's edge and stalling forever, or taking a chance and jumping to the beam and living as your healthiest and greatest self! Although there are many variations of mental muscle ups, here are my favorites to ensure they are always kept sharp and ready to deploy (should the need arise). These exercises are about **creating the habit** to use these tools in your day to day life, so they can be called on automatically in times of challenge, stress, or in the presence of toxicity.

Above all, it is my hope that in reading this book, it will remind you to be aware of your **power to choose** exactly what comes into your life, what stays, what has an effect on you (and in what way) and by using these tools, what you can do about it!

A Quick Tip Before You Begin:

So I know of a guy. He is what people like to call a 'Debbie Downer.' He has this uncanny ability to put a negative spin on anything around him, or anything that has happened in his life. I always found myself thinking he should get into risk management. In any situation, he has already thought of the worst case scenario, and what would need to be done should that crisis occur. Things that I would never have dreamed of happening, he has thought about and pictured in advance. In essence (and quite hilariously to me), he has legitimately prepared for any disaster known to mankind. If the zombie apocalypse ever materialized, I would head straight to his place.

But underneath it all, I can see he is unhappy. Whilst getting into the reasons why he feels this way are beyond the scope of this book, it is clear that he has developed the habit of thinking negatively. He has his 'negative filter glasses' on, and (as we will delve into a little later), habits are hard to break! To be honest, I don't think he realizes just how much of a Debbie

Downer he is, because this is the reality he has created to live in.

Maybe you know of someone similar to him (or maybe that someone is even you). If it is you, perhaps when trying to exercise **mental muscle ups,** you find it feels forced, or doesn't feel right. Don't give up, though! Similar to learning how to do a real muscle up (or any new activity), it may seem weird and awkward, and maybe you will fail it a few times. But keep practicing with a 100% commitment and you'll get there, no matter where you are right now. I'd be willing to bet my life on it!

You will not reach your **Fitness Utopia** (or any journey to greatness in your life), with a negative mindset, and hate in your heart. If you find yourself cycling through negativity due to a perceived failure in the past, and ruminating over these events, these muscle ups are great tools to help you progress. Add in the muscle up exercises below into your **Mind Diet** program and create the health and the life that you deserve!

Positivity Jam

Create a music file called The Positivity Jam. Fill it with music that makes you wanna get up and dance. To each their own, but I always found that something fast, upbeat and silly gets me going.

Now, dance as if no one is watching. I mean really go for it! Don't hold back. Shake that moneymaker, bump and grind, twerk and werk it like all of those big booty biyatches that you see on the Internet. If you are in a group setting doing this, everyone should get up and do it together. Be as silly as possible! Feels good right?

The Complimenter (Group)

One person (preferably someone who works well on the fly and is good at improvisation), will stand in the middle of the circle. Everyone around them will start clapping and making noise. Your silliest sounds are encouraged! Then, the person in the middle will start pointing at each individual in the circle, and giving them a compliment, After each compliment, everyone cheers. It works best when The Complimenter is fast at compliments, and the key is to say things that people may not expect. The Complimenter attempts to compliment as many as he can while the group claps and encourages.

G'Day Gratitude (Active)

Using a basketball hoop and ball, think of a thing you are thankful for then dribble up and shoot. (This can also be done with a soccer net and ball).

The title for this activity came about in the most roundabout way. Someone very nice was gifting me with a necklace, and it could be engraved with whatever I wanted on it. I wanted something original, special to me and something I could also identify with. I also wanted it to be a statement of how I lived my life.

The word G'day represents the easy going, happy, casual nature that most Australians embody. It's literal meaning is "Good Day" or "Hello". And we all know what gratitude means. But G'Day Gratitude is so much more than just saying thank you to someone.

In a very easy going, laugh at yourself kind of way, it's about truly being thankful for the gift of living, the gift of health and your ability to change it. To choose to express gratitude to create your life however you want by just giving it a go - because, why not?! It's about always being thankful for whatever happens to you. G'Day Gratitude is learning that everything that happens to you is the greatest thing. Because once you make the choice that it is, it will be!

Gratitude Apples (Group)

The group breaks into two teams. Each team has a wheelbarrow or bucket filled with water and apples. The group needs to get their apples from the wheelbarrow to the other side (at a distance) picking up the apples using only their mouths and running and dropping the apples at the other side. Water balloons can also be used!

Before attempting to pick up each apple, the person must say aloud what they are thankful for.

Appreciation Letter

Write a letter of appreciation to someone who has changed your life (or helped you in some way), and send it to them. For that extra gratitude (and if it's possible), schedule a visit to read it to them aloud. Tip: Don't tell them you are coming with a letter. Allow them to be surprised, and feel the energy of appreciation and how good it makes you both feel!

Gratitude Board/Jar

Create a vision board or jar. List and add everything that gives you gratitude. Color works wonders. Get creative!

Acceptance Muscle Up

I found the best way to practice your acceptance muscle up is to do yoga. Recently I decided to do a personal yoga challenge for 30 days. That's yoga everyday, for 30 days. It was to not only increase my skill set, but also to try something new and learn to fail.

I mentioned this before, but it's worth mentioning again. Yoga is wonderful for its lessons in the subject of acceptance. Once we fully accept where we are, we can then lean into those poses. The body will then work to move forward and find a solution to progress into more advanced poses. Without this acceptance, progression cannot occur.

Do yourself a favor and start yoga, either on your own and using the many classes or teachings available for free online today, or join a yoga studio. Whatever your fitness level, everyone can benefit!

Faith Muscle Up for Groups

This trust exercise requires some setting up before it can be executed. It also requires a large, open area such as a room without furniture (or an empty parking lot). The leader must distribute "mines," which they place haphazardly around the area. These "mines" can be balls, bowling pins, cones, etc.

Pair up with someone. This muscle up gives partners a chance to work on trust issues (which is why they are paired into teams of two). One person is blindfolded and cannot talk, and the other can see and talk, but cannot enter the field or touch their blindfolded partner.

The challenge requires each blindfolded person to walk from one side of the field to the other (which is endowed as their **Fitness Utopia**) by avoiding the placed objects by listening to the verbal instructions of their partners.

You have the option to make it a competition by tallying up each time a blindfolded person hits an object. But the real idea behind the game is to get the team members to trust their partner's directions, while also learning to communicate more effectively.

Blind Trust

This trust building exercise requires nothing more than a few blindfolds and a large, flat area (preferably with grass). Each person partners up, and chooses whether they are the leader or the follower in the first round. The follower puts on a blindfold.

The group leader then holds the hand of their blindfolded partner then:

1. Takes them on a slow walk around the area for at least 3 minutes.
2. Walks at a normal pace for at least 3 minutes.
3. Walks at a fast pace for at least 3 minutes.

Then, each leader and follower switches roles.

After the last round, stop and chat about what each person experienced. Was it difficult for participants to trust their partners and if so/not, why?

Look At MOI

This trust exercise requires no special equipment, just an even number of people. Making eye contact is sometimes difficult for some, as it requires a certain amount of trust and respect. In your own life, do you make eye contact when speaking to someone, or do you avoid it? Does it feel awkward or forced?

Although the exercise is simple, it's great for helping people become more comfortable with each other. It's also effective in building self worth and confidence. Any path to greatness will require, at some point, being seen. So you might as well start practicing!

For this activity, have people group into pairs and stand facing each other. The idea is to have them stare into their partner's eyes for at least 60 seconds. There may be some giggles at first, as it can feel somewhat awkward during the first try, but as participants get the hang of it, it should become easier for them to make eye contact for prolonged amounts of time.

Faith in Falling

This exercise takes me back to school camps. We did this often and I believe it's in the movie *Mean Girls.* The way it works: one person stands on a platform and falls into the crowd. The rest of the crowd catches them. I believe in *Mean Girls* they allow the person to fall, which makes the title of the movie fitting. Don't be a Mean Girl!

Trust Leans

This is another group exercise. One person volunteers to stand in the middle of the circle. They stand upright, eyes closed and their feet together. They then begin their 'trust leans', which involve swinging forward and backwards (and through different planes of motion) in the circle. The group should not allow them to fall, or feel frightened as if they're going to fall.

Safety Tip: Those in the circle must spot with one foot in front of the other, with their arms outstretched, elbows locked, and fingers loose and ready to catch the person performing their trust leans. This will ensure that they can successfully pass the person in the circle around without any trouble. Everyone in the circle takes a turn being in the middle, and the exercise should last about a minute each!

Tips on Scheduling Mental Muscle Ups

Perhaps you (or the fitness professional you have hired) has chosen a particular workout, or set of exercises that you need to do to move closer to your **Fitness Utopia**. Although two trainers working in a similar discipline may program similarly, there is no singular set path to success. Different strokes for different folks, folks! This is one of the reasons why you may prefer one personal trainer over another. Each has a different style, personality, and method to their madness.

The Mind Diet is the same. Consider yourself your own **Mind Diet** trainer, programming into your schedule the various individual exercises you'll need to get to your **Fitness Utopia** in the most efficient way. Map out a plan each week, and reassess every seven days if you feel something needs to be changed.

If you need some guidelines on a good place to begin, a general beginners guide could follow these principles:

- Choose a muscle up that helps to maintain your own individual strengths once a week. For example, you might have a very cheerful disposition, and already have established a great habit in training your mind to think positively. So, schedule a **mental move** based on this once a week: Wednesday you treat yourself to a one hour sauna/ steam session to keep those cheerful/joyful vibes going. Like all of the **little d's**, once they are scheduled, make them a priority, and don't deviate from these times.

- Choose a mental muscle up that aids in areas you are not as strong at but would like to improve on. Commit to focusing on these areas by completing these muscle ups two to three times a week. They can be different mental muscle ups, and can target different areas of your perceived focus points. For example, perhaps you would like to work on kindness, and also gratitude. To do this, you have scheduled volunteering at the animal shelter twice a week on Tuesday afternoons, and Sunday during the day. You have also scheduled every Thursday a night your 'Pay It Forward' night, where you do something nice for someone every week.

We will learn more about how to create winning habits in Chapter 7, but at this point, schedule these muscle ups into your calendar. Place them on repeat until you reach **The Big D.** I've always found it's easiest to place mental muscle ups on repeat indefinitely, and I can switch them up once I've reached my planned destination.

Once they are scheduled in your calendar, it is of utmost importance that you keep these commitments you've set, so you can begin to **create the habit** to execute your mental muscle ups *every week*. It's astounding what you can accomplish with a little consistency, and this is exactly how to do it!

The Lesson

Master your mental muscle ups by scheduling them regularly into your calendar.

Chapter 6

Become BFF's With Failure

We are all of us failures, - at least, the best of us are.
James M. Barrie

If you've browsed through any self help book before, and haven't been living under a rock for the last twenty years, I'm sure you've heard in some manner that you gotta be okay with failure to succeed in anything.

You would think that armed with this knowledge, we might be a little more supportive and forgiving of ourselves, (and of each other) when we attempt something at the risk of failure.

Sadly, this is not the case. We touched on this topic in Chapter 4, but I wanted to really delve into this head on by taking our relationship with failure (and our fear of it) to the next level. Deploying mental muscle ups in this area is so important, that I have dedicated this chapter to doing exactly that! Generally speaking, you may not initially get the support you need from others, so it's of paramount importance that your **faith muscle-up** is sharp; along with diligent homage to the **mental moves** that support your **3W.**

In addition to these things, it's beneficial to not only be okay with failure and your fear of it, but to become BFF's with your fear of it, and the event of a perceived failure itself. Because it's this fear (and what happens after an event of assumed failure), that can account for the reason so many of us are living our fears today, and not our dreams.

If you're into psychotherapy, then you may have learned that like most of your patterns, fear was learned at some point in your childhood. An event occurred that didn't go according to plan, or the plans of someone around you. When we are children, that someone (or someone's) were probably your parents, school friends, or family members.

Although there were many instances growing up that taught me this fear of failure, I think one of the defining events was when I applied as a teenager to go to a smarty pants high school. In Australia, we call these 'selective schools'. My mother was counting on me getting in; as she didn't approve of the local public high schools in the area. If I didn't get in, she wanted to send me to an expensive private school instead; which she would end up paying for out of pocket.

When I sat the test, I was twelve years old. And I didn't get admitted. To add salt to the wound, my childhood best friend got in. This was one of the very first times that I can remember feeling a real sense of shame and disappointment in myself. I tried out again the following year. On the day of the test, my mother told me not to tell anyone that I was sitting it. When I asked why, she said, "In case you don't get in, stupid!"

I didn't get in. Again.

Although there was no reason for her to say what she said in that manner, as an adult now I am able to see it from her perspective. She was hoping to avoid expensive private school fees, and it was her way of wanting to give me the best chance at a good education (and in her mind) a good life. But, I also see how her own shame and perfectionist tendencies were projected onto me due to competitiveness that existed between her and my best friends mother. It's well understood that children are an extension of their parents. Any failures on their child's part is mostly seen from both the parents (and others around them) as a direct reflection. Which may or may not be true! Trust me when I say that I am telling this story with love. Everything that has happened to me has made me who I am today, and I wouldn't change a single thing.

At the time though, I found myself harboring a profound sense of internal guilt, shame and disappointment in myself about not being who my mother wanted me to be. There was so much shame that I felt my failure to be too shameful to even talk about. I felt unworthy, and didn't think I should waste any additional time on my shortcomings as a person. As a result, I became terrified to do anything that I didn't know *for sure* I was good at. It is a pattern I am still unlearning to this day. I became a perfectionist in the dark, practicing things in secret till I knew I was great at them before I would attempt *anything* in front of others. If I tried something and failed, I kept it hidden away like a dirty secret, along with my shame and mental beatings from my inner hater.

I don't think you can come into your wisdom until you have made mistakes on your own skin and felt them in reality of your own life.
Elizabeth Gilbert

The Silver Lining

The thing I love about fitness is how much it has taught me about how to live life outside of the gym. In the gym, we learn that in order for our muscles to grow we need to tear them. In time, (and with consistency in tearing those muscles), they rebuild stronger in order to handle this new consistent, heavier load. The only way for these muscle tears to happen is we need to fail in the gym. Sweaty, awkward, I can't possibly do anymore. Maxed out. Every damn day.

In the gym, I learned that failure is a friend, not a foe. That if I became BFF's with failure and pushed past my fear of it, I'd see results. I learned that dancing on the edges of my own personal limits was exactly how my health was taken to the next level. I learned to trust in my body, and have confidence that it would know what to do, and look for a solution when under pressure. I created the habit to push myself to the limit in the gym. Over time, it actually felt uncomfortable to be there and half-ass a workout. Because it wasn't my habit anymore!

If hauling ass in the gym isn't your habit yet, don't worry. It wasn't mine at some point in my life either. But just like I have, you can take a deep breath, pick yourself back up and you can choose to write a new story. A story that allows you to live your dreams, instead of your fears. You can take all of those perceived failures you have experienced yourself firsthand, and instead of letting it burn away your self worth (and confidence) into ashes, you can use it as fuel to learning whatever lesson it is trying to teaching you. Because I guarantee a lesson is there!

The Deal

It's not that I'm so smart, it's just that I stay with problems longer.
Albert Einstein

Every winner has decided to become BFF's with their fear of failure (and the event of failure itself). Well, maybe not *exactly* BFF's, but they make peace with its presence, and accept it's unavoidable existence in their journey to greatness. So, recognize that it's your silver lining, even if it doesn't feel like it at the time. Although failure will never be comfortable, and living in the fear of failure isn't a party either, they are still gifts! They are signs from God, The Universe, or even Your greatest self in a parallel dimension trying to help you - **that something needs to change within you,** so you can move forward and rise up to be your best self.

Most of the time, it isn't the things we want to hear or see, because it will mean taking responsibility for our health (or our lives), and the way it is at this moment. As they say, the truth hurts, but first it will piss you off. Accept it, forgive yourself, and gain the wisdom you need from these events to try again, with an even bigger chance of moving forward. If you are standing on your mountains edge, contemplating your jump, of course it's going to be uncomfortable. Because you are just standing there, stuck. Jump! Trust that your body knows exactly what it needs to do to progress, whether you fly to the beam and continue on from there, or you miss you mark and fall, because there is something important down there that you are meant to find: A lesson, another approach, an awakening, or a even a complete redirection.

So in order to combat your fear of failure, (or move beyond an event of perceived failure), you need to start believing that you can change. That **you are worthy** of this change you are envisioning. That all humans can change and grow, and that human transformation can happen. By going through my own personal transformation, I have discovered that it is completely possible! I've also been blessed to witness so many transformations from my clients in health and fitness, and watch them blossom into their healthiest selves. But that's my reality that I've created over time. It didn't begin like that, but by going through a process that I'm proud to call **The Mind Diet,** I've made the changes necessary to create and maintain my reality in my **Fitness Utopia**.

What is the reality that you have chosen to live in? Do you believe you can teach an old dog new tricks? Do you believe every stumble you make along the way is an opportunity for you to grow, and begin again? Do you believe failure wakes you up to the things you weren't aware of; that **you would never have learned** if you didn't fail? Do you believe failure is happening in your favor (and as uncomfortable as it is), a crucial element in the journey to your best self?

> **I've missed more than 9000 shots in my career. I've lost almost 300 games. 26 times, I've been trusted to take the game winning shot and missed. I've failed over and over and over again in my life. And that is why I succeed.**
>
> **Michael Jordan**

Each day you have the power to wake up and to choose. You can decide whether to let an event of perceived failure define who you are as a person (and as a result), act accordingly thereafter within those parameters of failure. Or, you have the choice to stand up and say, "Wait a second. That's not me. That's not who I am." And you choose to create a new story and you try again. A story that works **against** the past event of perceived failure. You have a choice. You've always had it! And I get it… shit happens. If you're living on Earth today, shit has either already happened to you, or it's gonna happen real soon. But as I've said before, it's never about what happens anyway. It's what you do *about* what happens that makes all the difference.

So today, choose to create a new story. A story that supports living a life of your dreams, and not your fears. And armed with your best **mental muscle ups** (and all of the great tools that you'll learn about in **The Mind Diet**), you can walk confidently through your fear of failure and risk failing again, so you can live your success story instead. #CreateANewStory

The Mind Diet Mental Moves

On Becoming BFF's with Failure

> **Never let the fear of failure be an excuse for not trying. Society tells us that to fail is the most terrible thing in the world, but I know it isn't. Failure is part of what makes us human.**
>
> **Amber Decker**

If you are having trouble letting go of a past failure, or find yourself stuck on the edge of your cliff longer than you deem reasonable, here are some of my favorite exercises that you can add into your **Mind Diet** schedule; so you can keep moving forward towards your **Fitness Utopia** (and any journey to greatness in life).

Fear Factor

What is your greatest fear? Is it snakes, spiders, crocodiles? Is it singing out loud in front of a group, or standing in front of people naked? Reading your journal aloud or skydiving? Telling someone your deepest, darkest secret?

It's time to meet your biggest fear head on! This is a great exercise for groups. If it's a kind of sexual fear you want to realize though, there are probably plenty of *other* places you could do that: hint, hint - NOT HERE.) Whatever it is, make it your own, and choose something that you are legitimately terrified to do. Then do it. If you are in a group, do it in front of everyone. How do you feel?

Physical Feat

Although you may have already chosen something as part of your **3W**, this is a great exercise for challenging yourself to get out of your element, by doing something you wouldn't usually do. Ideally, it would be something easily organized. Perhaps it's 100 squats a day for 7 days. Maybe you head to the video arcades to challenge someone in various games, many of which can get quite physical. Maybe it's a 30 day yoga challenge!

I recently completed my own 30 day yoga challenge for this very reason. Yoga everyday, for 30 days. I think I've mentioned this previously, but yoga is not my strongest skill. I wanted to get comfortable being uncomfortable, being around a room full of people who were great yogis that could see me fail, and learn that I could survive it all and in fact come out better on the other side. As a result, I'm a lot better at yoga than I used to be!

The Chair Dump

This is similar to the exercise listed under the mental moves for self worth. However, you should instead visualize a defining memory where you felt the fear of failure (or you experienced what you define as a failure to you).

Alternatively, sit on one chair and practice stillness. When you feel calm, ask yourself why you are afraid to fail. What comes up? Who do you associate these feelings with? Then, without blame, associate these feelings with them. Leave the fear of failure (or the perceived event of failure behind on that chair), and choose to create a new story in the new chair.

Fear Diving

This can be done on your own or in a group. Sit down and quiet your mind. If you are in a group, one person sits across from you while the others can watch. The question is asked:

"Why are you afraid?"

With yourself or others, say what comes to mind. The question is continually answered You might find yourself getting deeper and deeper as to why you might be afraid, and eventually you may identify the root cause of your fear (which is often very different to your first answer). The aim is to find the root cause. From here, deploy another exercise (such as Cutting Ties or The Chair Dump), in order to let that go of that root cause, to create a new story.

The Lesson

My favorite part about getting older is realizing all the adults I looked up to were really just winging it.

Steve Maraboli

Failure and your fear of it is not going anywhere, so you might as well become BFF's with it. And despite what it looks like from the outside, everyone is really just winging it. Why not you too? #YouAreWorthy

Chapter 7

Habitually Fit

The second half of a man's life is made up of nothing but the habits he has acquired in the first half.

Feodor Dostoievski

My first meetings with new nutrition clients are always interesting, (yet slightly unnerving) adventures. I have each client write me a food log to get an idea of what they're eating. From there, I can determine how we can best proceed to make the changes they would like to make in their health.

I'll argue that it's in receiving these initial food diary logs that I can determine the mental mindset of that individual with more accuracy than if I was to chat with them directly about their goals. It is frightening, (yet hilarious) at how many people lie on their charts. I receive food logs that present the perfect picture of nutritional health. Yet the reason they are hiring me is for one of those general goals mentioned in Chapter 1. If in fact, they were eating a plan similar to what had been sent in their initial food log, I doubt their health would be in the place it is today and my services would not be needed.

But in order to see the changes physically on our body, and arrive at our personal **Fitness Utopia**, it requires a change in current behavioral habits. It is one of my fundamental beliefs that a person's physicality is a by-product of what is going on inside a person's mind. So if you want to change your body (and make those changes last), you need to first change your mindset. This includes looking at the fundamental beliefs and thoughts that shape your actions and habits today.

For example, perhaps you have the habit of replaying past mistakes over and over again in your head, such as the numerous times in the past that you've started going to the gym, then stopped. As a result the feelings of shame and failure from those experiences stop you from joining any gym currently, or exercising at all.

Perhaps you have a habit of worrying you're going to injure your knees when you squat, because it's what happened the last few times. So you never go to the gym and squat. And guess what? You never learn to squat correctly… and because you don't squat, your knees get even worse.

The stories that we accept as part of our identity, and stories we believe to be true have the power to mould and shape our reality as we see it. We might allow one perceived failure in the past to mould and shape our reality for the same, (or a very similar) event in the future. If we have allowed this perceived failure to take root in our subconscious mind, we will do this without even knowing we have done it. We do this in every part of our lives: our health, our relationships, our career - *everything.*

This can actually be a positive thing, if the story you are claiming as your reality adds to the growth and transformation of you into your best self.

But if it isn't, often a single, perceived random event of failure can have lifetime ramifications on a person. It can change the course of a person's future forever if these habits are not uncovered and exposed for the frauds that they are.

When I was a kid, I ran track and field. One day, when attempting a high jump, I launched from the ground to jump over it and I accidentally landed with my back on the bar. Beforehand, I had been decent at high jump. Although it definitely stung, I didn't hurt myself too much. No broken bones and no bruises!

After that single event however, I became very afraid to do high jump. I worked myself up into such a frenzy, worried I would land on my back again whenever I jumped. It took two weeks to muster up the courage to jump again. When I finally did, guess what happened?! You guessed it.

From then on, I decided I must be a horrible at high jump, and I chose to never do it again. And sadly, I never have. Knowing what I know now about habits and stories of perceived failure, I could have chosen to write a new story.

You too, can choose to write a new story. Can you think of anything that has happened in your life that has changed the way you behave and interact with the world?

> **If you raise your standards but don't really believe you can meet them, you've already sabotaged yourself. You won't even try; you'll be lacking the sense of certainty that allows you to tap the deepest capacity that's within you... Our beliefs are like unquestioned commands, telling us how things are, what's possible and impossible and what we can and cannot do. They shape every action, every thought and every feeling that we experience. As a result, changing our belief systems is central to making any real and lasting change in our lives.**
>
> **- Anthony Robbins**

A change in your behavioral habits is firstly brought about by a conscious change in your thoughts. Simply put: **if you want different results, you gotta think different things.** Because thoughts become things! If you work to consciously think these different things everyday, eventually these different thoughts will become part of your unconscious habits, and beliefs - and *voila*! A new habit is made, and you're on that express train to your **Fitness Utopia.**

There is a transtheoretical model (developed by James 0. Prochaska, Ph.D. & Carlo C. DiClemente, Ph.D in 1982), which categorizes *'The 5 Different Stages of Change'* an individual exhibits when attempting to change behavioral patterns. Whilst this model was created to better understand the behavior of how smokers give up their addiction to cigarettes, it is also useful in categorize the stage of changes in any type of behavioral habit: good or bad. It's a fairly accurate representation of the general stages you may experience when trying to drop a toxic behavioral pattern, (and essentially the unhealthy actions that go with it), to instill healthier alternatives that work in harmony with your **3W.**

Stage 1. Pre-Contemplation of Habits

This is usually the stage where I find most of my nutrition clients in. Although they have approached me to make changes, subconsciously they will sabotage themselves by their unwillingness to be honest on their log, and accept their

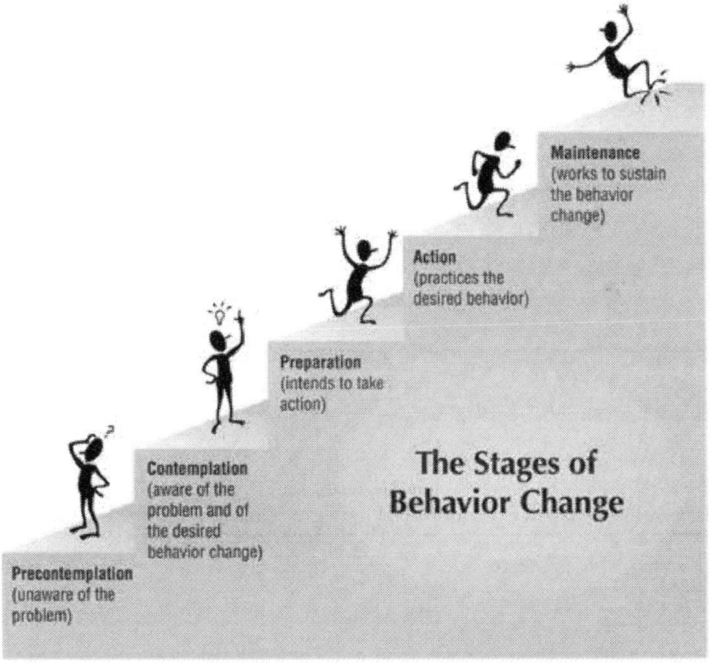

Sources: Grimley 1997 (75) and Prochaska 1992 (148)

situation for what it is. The answers on their food log show me they are *in denial* about their unhealthy habits, and/or are unwilling to see their problem listed so plainly on paper in front of them. It's just too much of the real deal. Information is filtered through selectively, and a victim mentality is often apparent. Do any of these sentences sound familiar?

"I have no idea what happened to me, I don't know why I put on so much weight!"

"It's my husband's fault, he shouldn't bring home Dunkin' Donuts everyday from work."

"I am just far too busy to have the time to workout and eat right."

"If I had time, I'd look like you!"

"I can't cook."

"I'm broke!"

"It's just one bite and one drink, what's that gonna do?"

"I don't have a gym membership and the closest gym is too far away anyway."

"There have been studies that show you that your genes create your body type, so it doesn't matter if you exercise or eat healthy or whatever. I have a big boned family, so I'm doomed!"

"Weight doesn't determine your health."

"I'm too old now."

"I've had kids, things change after kids."

Sigh.

It's honestly heartbreaking to see so many block themselves from the blessing of how good their body is designed to feel. Although they are different statements, all sentences share a common thread: that each person is un-willing to accept **complete responsibility** for their own health and fitness, and the habits they execute to have gotten them there. They are also unwilling to change those toxic beliefs and habits that will essentially change their bodies, and transform their entire lives.

What has happened, has happened. Make peace with it, forgive yourself, take responsibility for yourself and your life, so you can then move forward.

- Oprah

I am a horrible yogi. But I love yoga for one of it's greatest teachings. And that is the concept of accepting yourself in this very moment and everything that makes you, **you.**

In a class, there are many around me in advanced poses, legs behind their head (or in positions I think I would otherwise see in a bondage torture chamber). It can be easy to get frustrated, or embarrassed that I am not where they are. I could also try and fake it till I fall flat on my face. I'll admit that like many of you, I'm a great faker. But I can never do it for too long. The cracks start to show. Plus, while I'm spending all of my energy on faking it, I'm not personally progressing from the true place I should be working from. The place from which I will genuinely progress, and the place that can lead me to my ultimate goal: my **Fitness Utopia.**

However, if I surrender, and accept the un-comfortability of where I'm at without shame. If I am honest about where I am at in each pose (and in my practice), I am able to then lean into these poses. From there, the path of my own progression into more advanced poses appears in a very natural, flowing, progressive, and predestined fashion.

You will never create new healthy habits if you cannot be honest, and *accept the existence* of your current unhealthy ones. Usually an emotional trigger, (or an event) will need to occur for a person to wake up, take responsibility and accept their situation for what it is. Perhaps your Doctor told you to change. Maybe you finally got on the scale and didn't like what you saw. Perhaps you are reading this book.

The lesson? Wherever you go, there you are. So accept, and surrender. Accept it fully for what it is, and just like Oprah has said, "…forgive yourself, so you can then move forward."

Stage 2. Contemplation of Habits

Have you ever been to those kids playgrounds at the park, and often they have a tiny little horse that's attached to a big spring? The spring makes the horse swing back and forth to large degrees, but the horse never travels anywhere. It's stuck in the playground.

If you're in Stage 2, I'm imagining that you are riding that horse as a fully grown adult in the playground. And it's okay and acceptable for a little awhile. Hell, it's even fun! But after awhile, if you stay on there - you start to look silly, and duh, you never go anywhere.

Overthinking is the thief of progress.

Welcome to the Contemplation stage. If you have gone through reading this entire book without doing any of the steps *yet*, newsflash! You are in the Contemplation stage, still deciding whether the struggle of instilling new healthier habits are worth the fight to exchange them for your older, toxic ones. Your unhealthy habits are under attack, and they are fighting hard to keep everything at the old status quo. They are best mates with overthinking, indecision and self sabotage. Even reading this book has them rallying together and ready to go to war!

Your quick fix? I always find that mediating on my **why** is helpful if I find myself wanting to stick to an old unhealthy habit; or any habits that don't work in harmony with my **what;** even though I've been given an opportunity to **jump** and change it. Remembering **when** is also helpful in minimizing analysis paralysis, so you can act *right now, in this moment,* and you aren't putting the task of changing your unhealthy habits in the, 'someday pile for someday.'

Additionally, visualization or doing the exercises that are your best triggers for action are useful from progressing from bad habits to good ones. When a plan is only as good as its execution, you can have all the answers in the world. But until you **jump,** until you do it: there you are, rocking back and forth on that kids horse in the playground, putting your dreams and fitness goals aside for someday. Ya feel me?

P.S. You look ridiculous. Get off.

Stage 3. Preparation of Habits

A goal without a plan is just a wish.

Execution of Steps 1-3 of **The Mind Diet** fall under this stage. If you are in Stage 3, setting your calendar up with ***The Big D*** and forecasted **little d's** along the way, you are well on your way to *creating new, healthier habits* that last, and will propel you forward to your **Fitness Utopia**. Because the best way to have success (not only in health, but in any area of your life), is to prepare for it!

Stage 4. Action of Habits

We are what we repeatedly do. Excellence is not an event, but a habit.

Now, as this chapter is about instilling habits that create and maintain a habitually fit *you,* Stage 4 and Stage 5 are most relevant in the habit making arena. Congratulations if you've made your first **jump** of Step 4 of **The Mind Diet**. This is the *only way* to begin a new habit. You've pushed past fear, doubt and other evil forces to take your chance at flight. We don't stop there though! To make it a lasting change on your healthy habits, there needs to be a consistent, conscious action of multiple **jumps** that move you towards your **little d's** and ultimately **The Big D**. In short, *you need to create the habit to always jump* when the opportunity is there. Winners recognize that it is the multiple jumps throughout their life that they've taken that has separated them from the pack, and defined them as the winners they are today.

Let's go back and look at our good friend Becky and her specific fitness goal. With her **3W** in mind, I have listed examples of new habits she can execute to create new, conscious healthier habits that help her get to her goal.

BECKY

WHAT: Ten pound weight loss

WHEN: Two months

OLD UNHEALTHY HABIT	NEW HEALTHY CONSCIOUS HABIT	HEALTHY SUBCONSCIOUS HABITS
Becky would eat cake at the office whenever there was a birthday	Becky politely refuses from now on, because she has her wedding coming up. She instead has a stash of healthy protein bars, and whenever there is a birthday, she will eat one of those instead of the cake.	Becky doesn't even want cake because she works too hard to blow it all away on some sugar. Sometimes, she might have a bite but generally the cake seems too sweet for her.

Becky loves going out for Friday night work drinks	Becky stopped going out for Friday night drinks completely for 3 weeks, even though she felt like she missed out on some good times and workplace gossip. For those 3 weeks,she scheduled a spa treatment each Friday instead to reward herself for not boozing up. After the initial 3 weeks, she felt strong enough to go there and not have any alcohol, because she was feeling really good and didn't want to ruin the progress she was finally seeing. Plus, her wedding was now only 5 weeks away and she was down 6 pounds already!	Becky can't go for Friday night drinks because she is training for a triathlon, and they have scheduled ride every Saturday. She doesn't really mind because she finds out all the workplace gossip on Monday, and she really enjoys the company of her triathlon group - who are also great at gossiping.
Becky would be too tired after work sometimes to go to the gym when she was scheduled to go	Becky changed her workout schedule to the morning and scheduled it into her calendar. She didn't like getting up early but she knew she needed to, because she wouldn't go at the end of the day and losing an hour or so of sleep was so worth it when she could envision herself in her wedding dress, walking down the aisle.	Becky is in a regular routine where during the week her alarm is set to go off so she gets up and goes to the gym like she goes to work everyday. She doesn't even think about it anymore. She has created the habit.
Becky took the advice of her unhealthy best friend that that hated the gym and was "naturally skinny". Her friend said she was working out too much and was overtraining.	Becky has a program and nutrition plan designed for her by a fitness professional. She trusts this fitness professional knows what is best for her body and her results, even if it contradicts with the advice of her best friend.	Becky politely thanks her best friend for her advice and offers to refer her onto her own fitness professional who she thinks could help her best friend.

Stage 5. Maintenance

In this model, Stage 5 is defined as sustained successful lifestyle modification. The hard work of changing habits has been completed. New, healthy habits are in place and the older habits can seem unnatural and futile to a person that has successfully arrived or is well on their way to their **what.**

Referring to the example of Becky, the table above shows how a conscious, consistent, (and usually uncomfortable) set of **jumps** or changes in her actions (at the start of her fitness journey in the first column), has created the subconscious shift over time to naturally embody those healthy habits consistently in the third column. As she has created this healthy habit, she will now subconsciously move away from any of the unhealthy actions and habits of her old self. Great success!

Habits, once created, are hard to change, whether they are good or bad. By nature, humans are resistant to change, even if we know that a change in our habits is in our ultimate best interests! An *astronomical* level of energy, faith and continual conscious effort over time is required to uproot any habit, then replace it with another one that contradicts the former. The time taken is highly variable and dependent on each person. It can depend on an individual's personal level of motivation, their level of honesty and acceptance, willingness to change, their current fitness and health level, and what specific habit they would like to change.

Okay, calm down. I can feel you freaking out through the cosmos. The good thing is, whilst it is very difficult, it is also **completely possible!** I am a living, breathing and working example of a person who has made a change in habits, health, body and lifestyle. Knowledge is power! In knowing this, now *you can choose* to make the changes necessary.

Step 5: Create The Habit

It is our choices that show us who we are, far more than our abilities.
- J.K. Rowling

If I'm doing it and Becky is doing it, then this means all the cool kids are doing it. So that means you gotta do it too! It's time to drink your honesty serum. Make that a double shot if it will help you to do it faster. Half the battle is simply recognizing and accepting what particular habits of yours need to be kept, and which ones you need to let go of.

In the following table, write down every unhealthy, destructive habit you can think of that hinders your journey to your **what** in the left column below. On the middle column, write down how this habit can be changed to work in line with your **what** and **why**. In the third column, list something you can do right now to change these habits. **(Jump!)**

MY UNHEALTHY HABITS	A HEALTHIER ALTERNATIVE	MY JUMP / EXERCISES

The Mind Diet Mental Moves

On Exercising Good Habits

The Balloon Drop

This exercise involves endowing helium balloons to release toxic habits that do not support your greater good. Additionally, *The Balloon Drop* can be useful in letting go of toxic entities outside of yourself, such as other people.

1. Write each of your unhealthy habits/toxic entities on each balloon. You can also grab your workout buddies and do *The Balloon Drop* together. This can be a fun, cathartic group exercise!

2. In a circle, each person takes their turn standing in the middle. Speak of how each particular endowed balloon has stopped you from stepping into your best self, in health and/

or life. Dwell on the weight of what each balloon represents. If you are doing this exercise alone, I find it better to speak out aloud as if people were there.

3. When you are ready to let go of each balloon, repeat this sentence: "Today, *I choose* to release the need for this in my life."

4. Then let go and release. Feels good, doesn't it?

The Squat Alarm

This can be done either by yourself or with a group. It's also a great exercise to do in an office. Set some alarms on your phone. Choose a sound that is different from your ringtone (or anything else.)

This sound is hereby known as *The Squat Alarm.* You can also get another person to set your alarms so you are unaware of when the alarms are going to go off.

When they do go off, you and your group must stop whatever they are doing, and complete fifty squats. Whatever your group is doing, upon hearing the sound you must drop it low for 50 repetitions. It can be a hilarious activity in the office and loads of fun if everybody gets involved!

The aim is for you and your group to associate this alarm with exercise. In time, you can use this sound to indicate it's time for your workouts at the gym or whatever activity you have chosen. This is especially awesome for those early morning workouts. Once you train your brain to associate that chosen sound with fitness and health, it will be easier than you think to get up and get your butt to the gym - because you've created the habit to do so!

Your Mind Diet Mutual Motivator

A great way to keep healthy habits is to choose a *Mind Diet Mutual Motivator.* Your *Mind Diet Mutual Motivator* is exactly like having a workout partner, but better! It is someone who *ideally* has read **The Mind Diet** and is familiar with its principles on programming, and has had some success with instilling habits that have resulted in sustained change. Your *Mind Diet Mutual Motivator* will be considered one of your cheerful entities that support your journey to success (more on cheerful entities in

Chapter 9).

You don't need to be of a similar physical shape to your *Mind Diet Mutual Motivator* for you to both be great match for each other. What is of utmost importance however, is for your commitment level to be the same. And by the same, I mean both of you are committed to keeping it 100%. Your *Mind Diet Mutual Motivator* will have a copy of the program you have designed for each calendar month in advance. You can choose to also have a copy of theirs. Each day, you will both check in and hold each other accountable for what you have set out to do.

You Can Do It!

When I was 18 years old, my staple diet consisted of 2 minute ramen noodles a few times a day. I broke that monotony up with entire blocks of chocolate eaten as my dinner. I ate mud cake, or Nutella on toast for breakfast. Often! Looking back, my face looked like it had been stung by bees because of all the sodium I ate on a daily basis. But I didn't know any better.

I also felt like absolute crap, but the way I felt was 'normal' for me at that point, so I didn't think too much of it.

Genetically, I am also allergic to alcohol, but in Australia, (a country that defines its culture in having a few beers anywhere, anytime), it was just not convenient to be allergic. Because it was habitual to do so, I would drink as much as everyone else, even though there was a high chance I would faint in public due to the allergy (which happened many times, but that's another story.) You don't need to be a rocket scientist to know that this was not a habit I executed with my best interests in mind.

Today, I am the oldest I have ever been while also being in the best shape I have ever been in. At an age of… well, I'm no spring chicken, let's just say that. But I have never felt better physically. People ask me, what do you do to stay in shape like that? And I could talk about specific exercises, and squats, and meal plans, and macronutrients, and fitness competitions, and marathons. But the semantics don't really matter. Because the real answer is this:

I created the habit to live my life in my Fitness Utopia.

And just like you might be doing now, I started in a place that was a world away from where I currently am. I struggled and fought through many conscious actions to change when everything inside of me did not want to. I battled through injury, lack of sleep, no motivation, depression, ridiculous work load, money troubles, fuck-boys and breakups. But I made it! And so can you.

Today it's not all smooth sailing, but this is life, remember? It ain't perfect, pumpkin. But in the Maintenance phase, it's not nearly as difficult as you might think it is. Because now my unconscious healthy habits are always working keep me in my **Fitness Utopia**, it would be just as hard for me to regress back to my original fitness level. This would mean creating a new habit, and I've already shown you how difficult that can be. So sometimes I skip the gym. Sometimes I go out and get drunk, and end up at gay bars tipping strippers in their jocks. But in the big scheme of things, it won't matter. I'm in the habit of doing the right thing most of the time, and habits are hard as hell to break!

The Lesson

In fitness, I've got some good habits. **That's all**. So can you.

Chapter 8

Some Next Level Shit

Every next level of your life will demand a different you.
- Leo DiCaprio

If you've gotten this far along and given **The Mind Diet** an honest run, then I'm so proud of you! You've taken a chance, left the ground, and taken the jump towards your best self. You've visualized what your **Fitness Utopia** looks like, and you have your visualization exercises and appropriate reminders scheduled in your calendar. You've exercised letting go of the habits that do not support your journey, and you think of your **why** whenever temptation presents itself. It may feel messy and uncomfortable at times, but finally you are feeling some sense of routine in your new healthy habits. Congratulations!

Now that you have a sense of the basics, it's time to take it to the next level. "But I've already taken it to the next level Edwina!" I hear you mutter. And believe me, I get it. No sooner do we get comfortable, that it's time to jump again.

But that's the whole thing about health and fitness, and really anything in life. If you ain't pushing yourself to go to that next level doing some next level shit, then there you are, back on that kids horse riding in the playground. Contemplating, yet not growing. Stuck in your own personal Stage 2 in 'The Model Of Change'. At this crucial time in your journey where the tables have been overturned, it's even more important we build on the momentum you've pushed so hard to create. Get comfortable feeling uncomfortable people, those jumps to the highest beams are never smooth rides! That's why there is hardly anyone out there.

Get Anally Specific

So let's go back to your **Fitness Utopia** and your **what/s.** By now, you have a very specific set of **what/s** in mind. So, it would only be fitting that you would also have a specific program, or a set of **jumps** and actions to support your journey to your **when/s,** and eventually **The Big D.** We covered the importance of scheduling in Chapter 3, and you have everything mapped out to succeed. Now that you are on your way, I wanted to touch on the topic of discovering your **strength in the specifics.**

One of the great things about **The Mind Diet** is it's ability to work in conjunction with any nutrition or strength and conditioning program. Perhaps you have hired a Personal Trainer or a Sports Nutritionist to help with your goals. Maybe you prefer yoga to CrossFit. Maybe you are Vegan, or Paleo, or you have just been diagnosed with diabetes. Whatever you have decided to be on this journey, whomever you have hired, whatever method you have chosen to have in your toolbox to your **Fitness Utopia** - be all there! I cannot stress this point enough.

Wherever you go, whatever you do, never half ass it. Always use your full ass.

I know some Vegetarians that eat meat secretly. I know some Vegans that get drunk every weekend and most of their meals are just french fries. I know some diabetics that go on sugar binges. Newsflash, people! If you are finding you are a Vegetarian that eats meat three times a week for example, then maybe it's time to reassess your specifics. How are you meant to know whether a certain method works for you best if you are hell bent on being half assed about it? And we make mistakes - we're human! We screw up sometimes and that's ok. It's important to forgive yourself and to always keep moving forward. But that's not what I'm talking about in these cases, though.

I'm referring to repeat, intentional actions that aren't in harmony with the plan or methodology you have chosen. Repeat actions that essentially hinder achieving your **what.** Every half assed effort results in an exponential loss in momentum. The momentum you worked so hard to create, remember?

You see, it never really matters the method you take at this stage. Just have the decisiveness to choose, and choose with conviction. Then set your personal parameters up, and *stick to it.* If you change methods, change completely and commit to the new method. You'll find your strength in the specifics!

… Psst… Wanna Know A Secret?

Once you see what specific targeted effort on a consistent basis does, you might become aware of a secret that all outliers or winners have learned to be true:

Most people half ass everything.

While so much of this behavior is a habitual by-product of an individual and their self worth, we can start to change this by conscious commitment. So whatever style of nutrition or exercise program you have chosen, **commit to it using your whole ass.**

There is so much strength, progress and enjoyment to be gained in simply showing up, and being all there. Give something your continual full attention to detail, and over time I promise you'll find your edge within those specifics. "But I'm so uncoordinated and I'll never be good at it!" you may say. Take a chance and show up everyday and use your whole ass. You just might surprise yourself. What have you got to lose by trying? Have your 50%, 45%, 75% or even 99% efforts been working for you so far? Exactly! There is that saying that madness is doing the same thing and expecting different results. If your current level of commitment hasn't been working so far, take a chance and try something new.

I see it everyday with my clients that are attempting a new PR. They begin very doubtful of their ability. Fast forward to a mere two weeks later, and they are surpassing that PR like it's a cakewalk. In my opinion, this is one of the most underrated **jumps** you can make that will set your full, peachy ass apart from the majority population. Show up on a consistent basis for your health and fitness, commit to the process you have chosen and it will be **easier than you think** to push for your edge.

Important note: Keeping your health and fitness on track is hard enough, so for goodness sake choose something you like the most and enjoy. For example, don't choose surfing if you hate the water, and you are deathly afraid of sharks. Don't choose the gym if it makes your skin crawl walking into the place every morning. That's the whole key to this fitness and health thing. Find something you like, (or for those fitness haters out there), choose an activity you hate the least, then get super-duper, anally specific about it. **Jump... using your whole ass.**

Often I have new clients approach me to train them, coming from other studios or fitness professionals. They are discouraged because their last fitness professional was a bodybuilder, and they wanted more of a yoga style program. But within two weeks I discover it isn't the style of training that is blocking them from achieving results; it's the halfway in, halfway out approach that's giving them (you guessed it), halfway results. That's one of the great things about health and fitness though and something I've always loved about it. It's fair. Whatever you put into it, you will get out of it!

Once you take charge, and take responsibility for your own commitment, you might surprise yourself with how fast you are progressing - no matter how you choose to move your body or what you decide to put in your mouth. It will literally astound you what a little consistency and an authentic, genuine commitment can do for you. In health and fitness, an effort and commitment of 100% will give you a 100% return on results. I'm no stockbroker, but that rate of return is pretty amazing, huh?.

When you're halfway in and halfway out, you'll always feel torn.

Now, there are times where you realize the activity that you were using as your vehicle to exercise is not the most efficient mode of transportation to achieving your **3W.** Perhaps, for example, you are powerlifting but your main fitness goal is to be able to do the splits and other Cirque De Soleil movements. So you're just cruising into your workouts until your current membership expires, and you can go and start ballet. But if you're in the gym 'half-assing' your powerlifting:

- Your glutes will hate you, because powerlifting creates thick peachy glutes, and this would have been the perfect time to build them.

- You'll become a half-assed powerlifter that can't do the splits.

- You'll have created a wonderfully toxic habit to half-ass **all** of your health and fitness pursuits which will probably make you a half assed ballet dancer. (If you need to go back and re-read the last chapter to recall how hard it is to change your habits, be my guest.) #OhSnap

But let's say you take a chance, and you commit yourself to powerlifting. You show up on time for training, and get lost in the details of hand placement, breathing techniques or learning how to perfect a power clean. You still may not be able to do the splits, but you'll become a kick ass powerlifter and you would have learned a lot about your body; along with skills that you can take into your next activity: ballet class! This is the human body, guys. Whichever way you choose to move or use it in fitness; whichever style of nutrition resonates best with you: a solid practice in one discipline *will always* compliment another discipline, no matter how different they look from the outset.

Step 6: Find Your Strength In The Specifics

#NextLevelYourNextLevel

List down some of the regular activities you might do on your path to **The Big D** on the left column. On the right column, write down how you can take this activity to the next level. This activity does not need to be only what you do in the gym or in the kitchen. It's any **jump**, physical or otherwise, that can be progressed to speed up your journey to **The Big D**. For reference, I have added in some examples of my own.

Specific Activity	Next Level Specific	When	Result
My weekly meal preparation	I will weigh out my food in advance that I have cooked and pack them into meals so I am not rushing everyday to put them together	Every Sunday	DONE
Leg Day Deadlifting	Add another plate on either side	Hump Day	Was able to do one plate. scheduling another plate next week
I will add another abs routine into my weekly workout	Program created with sets and reps. Doing at start of workout	Friday	
Steering Away From Negativity	I don't engage with the guy who is always saying I train too much		

#NextLevelShit

Specific Activity	Next Level Specific	When	Result

#NextLevelShit

Specific Activity	Next Level Specific	When	Result

Your list of specifics should be never ending, and you should always have the next task ready to be completed and scheduled. **Create the habit** to always take your next level to the next level, (or deepen your level of joy or enjoyment at the current level you're at). It's these nitty gritty, everyday, tiny actions or jumps that take us to our destination. It's all small stuff guys, but #duhBecky, the small stuff makes up the big stuff! And if you're anything like me and to-do lists, there is nothing more satisfying than writing lists and being able to check off that they are done. It also seriously tickles my fancy looking back and seeing how all of my small, day to day extra efforts have helped immeasurably in getting to my goal.

> **You never know whats around the corner. It could be everything. Or it could be nothing. You keep putting one foot in front of the other, and then one day you look back and you've climbed a mountain.**
>
> **- Tom Hiddleston**

Most people never believe me now, but I suffer from a tragic genetic condition called *'Flat Asian Booty Syndrome'*. It was passed down from my Dad, who is of Chinese heritage. I was sadly born with a butt very similar to the look of a pancake. As I am constantly fighting genetics, it takes a lot of targeted work to have built, and now retain my gluteus maximums. I hit legs three times a week, which may seem extreme for some people - but for me, it's what I need to do to make and retain changes. If I miss a session, they shrink. I'm not making this up. Now, if people ahem, check out my ass, I would argue they don't see what I see. They see a girl who's got an ass. And yeah, I've got an ass. But to me, it's more than that. The tip of the peach, if you will.

When I think of having a booty, I think of these small specific steps that I've taken above. Doing whatever I could do to take my next level to the next level in this area. I think of the hundreds of thousands of squats I've taken, sweaty and uncomfortable under a heavy barbell. I think of myself walking into the gym, not wanting to be there but knowing I had a goal to achieve and pushing through. I think of the many times I've said no to dessert, because I'd already hit my calorie count for the day. I think of having to let people go that didn't understand my lifestyle, my goals, my dream for greatness, and subsequently were toxic to my space, values and my boundaries.

When people look at just my gluteus gains and overall transformation, they only see the physical by-product of my mental transformation. I'd argue they are ultimately missing the best thing about it. And that's **the person I had to become to have it,** and the person I continue to become to keep it.

The Self Sabotage Monster

Although we touched on this topic briefly, I wanted to bring it up again as it pertains to specifics and taking your next level to the next level. It's like we are back again on that mountains edge, wondering if we should **jump**. We've jumped before, but maybe this time it will be different. Maybe this time you'll fall. Maybe you've reached your annual quota of **jumps** for the year. I mean who do you think you are? You've already made some waves and gotten some results. People are going to start thinking you're a narcissist with all that time you spend at the gym. There's no need to rock the boat any further!

Self sabotage is a bitch. It creates limits that aren't even there and stops you from stepping into your greatness and everything you were put on Earth to be. Stop and think for a moment. Can you recall a specific time you have sabotaged your journey to your **Fitness Utopia** previously? How could you have approached this differently, or what could you do the next time a situation similar to this rolls around?

SELF SABOTAGING EVENT/ BEHAVIOR	HOW I COULD HAVE CHOSEN A DIFFERENT PATH

You might notice your self sabotaging behaviors have been listed in Chapter 7 as they are or were a part of your habits. Many of the exercises I've listed already in **The Mind Diet** are great for slaying self sabotage for the snake that it is. Here is a quick summary of the general steps you might take to keep your mind sharp, and less likely to succumb to the toxic energy of self sabotaging impulses when they occur.

- Identify the self sabotaging behavior. Because if ya don't know, ya can't grow.
- Think of what specific events or occurrences led to you triggering this self sabotaging impulse. Map out the pattern, and try and think of as many circumstances as you can where this has happened to you in the past.
- Choose a new pattern. Now that you have identified with this toxic pattern, how can you respond differently the next time an impulse of this nature occurs?
- As we have talked about in Chapter 7, habits are formed by a conscious change in thoughts and following through with conscious action that works to help move you towards your **Fitness Utopia.** So make the choice to consciously walk this new pattern. by scheduling some time during the week to work on solidifying it into your life. It will be part of

your habits before you know it!

My Own Story of Self Sabotage

One of my most prominent examples of self sabotage happened when I was preparing for my first fitness competition. I had been in prep mode for 5 months. I started in November and even prepped over Christmas time and into the New Year when I went home to Australia for the holiday season. Having a Fijian mother means the family home is always packed with the most delicious and decedent food known to mankind. Enough to feed five Fijian football teams at a moments notice!

But I wasn't even interested in indulging and ruining my progress. I was scheduled to fly to Florida to see my coaches in person the following February (for a final camp) so I could be given the go ahead to compete and start my show circuit for that year. For 5 months, I was meticulous, and anally specific with my training and nutrition. I survived a trip to the other side of the world in the most festive holiday season of the year intact without a scratch. No stone was unturned, and everything was right on target.

Three days before I was scheduled to fly out, I sabotaged my preparation. I drove to Crumbs Cupcake Bakery in Los Angeles and I completely lost my mind. I have never seen anything like it (and I'm sure the people at the bakery hadn't either). I'm pretty sure I had a kid in tears because I was scaring everyone. If you've ever tried a Crumbs cupcake, you'll know it's not a normal cupcake. It's like a fuel injected cupcake, a super-duper steroid sized, rich as fudge, slice of heaven. One Crumbs cupcake is the equivalent of two and a half, or even three regular sized cupcakes. I completely demolished 4 Jumbo sized Crumbs Cupcakes, on my own, *before I'd even left the store.* Then I bought 4 more to take home with me.

I wasn't hungry. Anyone who has been on a competitor diet knows we eat approximately twice the amount of food as a regular person. I was eating 6 times a day, drinking two protein shakes, *as well* as a gallon of water a day. I was as fit as I had ever been up until that point. But I was about to fly across the country and do something I'd never done before. I was already getting bombarded with comments about my changes from work colleagues, friends, and my boyfriend at the time. Anyone that witnessed my transformation firsthand had something to say about it, and the majority of the comments were about me needing to be careful, to not take it too far, or that I looked really skinny. I was sent articles on metabolic damage, pleading with me to exercise caution because of this reason or that.

I was caught between following the advice of my new coaches located remotely across the country, or listening to the people I knew standing right in front of me who were all trying to get used to this 'new' me, (all of whom had never competed in a fitness competition before). To add fuel to the fire, it was my first competition and my inner hater was working on overdrive. Deep down, I worried I wasn't good enough, and I had no business standing on a stage in a bikini. I worried I wasn't pretty enough. I worried I was becoming too obsessed. I worried people would laugh at me onstage. I worried I would fall over in those five inch competition heels they make you wear. I worried I was becoming unbalanced. I worried I was making myself sick.

So I sabotaged my preparation. Afterwards, in a world of

stomach pain (and also the crushing feeling of regret that 5 months of solid work had been ruined in just 30 short minutes), I called my boyfriend up and told him what I'd done. He asked me why I had done it. I replied that I didn't know. Because at the time, I really didn't. I wasn't set up with the tools to be able to recognize a self sabotaging impulse when it appeared. I didn't know what I could have done beforehand to prevent it from occurring.

But today I know better, and with this wonderful awareness, I am able to see other areas in my life that I have also blindly self sabotaged. Much of the reasons we self sabotage is tied up in issues of self worth and self love. I'll delve into those things a little later. But hopefully through my stories, experiences and my lessons, you'll be able to recognize those impulses in your own life when they happen, and not have any YOLO trips to the bakery.

The Deal

When you give 50%, 65%, 80%, even 95% to your health and fitness journey, you are self sabotaging. Robbing yourself blind of being the best person you can be. So respect the time you have allocated in your schedule for your health and fitness, and show up for the specifics. Make every rep, and every movement count. Be all there with your whole heart, and get lost in the details. That means no phone ins. No sick days if you ain't sick. 100%. Every. Damn. Day.

Strength in the specifics is not just about the intensity of your workouts, or following your meal plan to a tee. There are some days that I am able to lift more than others, or I am faster one day and not the next. That's all part of it!

But what I'm talking about is the strength of your commitment, and *always keeping it 100.* It's about your commitment to always be pushing for a path to take your #nextleveltothenextlevel in every activity you do. It's about the showing up for the specifics in your **3W,** having the discipline to refer to those specifics everyday, and only walking a path that supports those specifics. It's about developing your strength and courage to say no to anything that deviates from that path, when my general guess is you haven't before (or you haven't with enough consistency to make lasting noticeable change). It's about putting in the time to master your chosen craft or method to your **Fitness Utopia.**

When I was just starting out, I didn't have any of these factors in place. I was running on pure motivation and first time steam, which we all know expires eventually. In hindsight and knowing what I do now, it's quite predictable that I ended up at the bakery. Using **The Mind Diet** would have given me the tools in place to allow me to reach **The Big D** with success. It was like I was going to war for the first time, but I decided to leave all of my armor and my weapons at home!
#AmateurMove

The Lesson

Create the habit in your health to #NextLevelYourNextLevel.

You'll find your strength in the specifics!

Chapter 9

The Power of No.

No's are bridges. Not walls. They will eventually be what gets you to the other side.
- The Angry Therapist

Every human went through a defining period when they learned how to say no. Do you remember when you started to say no? And through your innocent comprehension as a child, you first discover your right to choose.

Most babies learn the concept of no (and their power to choose), before they've learned how to say the actual word "no." It's a very important concept in a child's development. It's where they begin to conceptualize their own personal space and boundaries. Have you ever hung out with a kid who's just learned how to say no? You might notice that everything they say is no. It's a big **no** party! It's also the best kind of no party, because they couldn't give two hoots if saying no is not what you want to hear. They simply say no if they feel like saying no, and you just need to deal with it!

As we grow however, our natural need to be accepted and liked by others begins to overtake our (somewhat selfish) need to say no. Somewhere along the line, we learn that pleasing others gets us love and attention. Or to phrase it another way: we learn that not doing what others want you to do causes a withdrawal of love and attention.

Think back to a time as a kid when your parents got mad at you for doing something they didn't want you to do. Through your elementary understanding, it may have seemed like they withdrew love from you because they were mad. So, you stopped doing whatever naughty thing they deemed you were doing. They weren't mad anymore and the love returned. Call it discipline, call it whatever you want: a pattern is formed.

From a young age, we learn if we don't do what people around us want us to do, it will stop love. As our caretakers who clothe, feed and bathe us, this can seem very scary! As a result, we begin to surrender for our survival, and start to say yes to others against our own impulses.

While this change in habit is done as we grow up to be able to live in a socially acceptable (and functional) way in the world with others, I do believe that once the habit to be accepted and liked is learned, we can also find ourselves subconsciously just saying yes to many things. Things that we had no business saying yes to! At the expense of yourself, your health, your **3Ws** and your values.

Being natural people pleasers, women are more pre-dispositioned to do this than men. For my ladies reading this, perhaps you can recall a relationship where you didn't exercise your *Power of No* as much as you probably could have. Things can get a little more fabulously complicated when you throw in issues of self worth too. Because if some part of you does not believe you are worthy of love, you will always be seeking a way to earn it, and one way to do so is by pleasing others, and always saying yes.

When your friend drags you along to some shit you didn't want to do.

Have you ever been the cat in the following picture? Think back to a time when you agreed to do something, but if you really thought about it - it wasn't what you wanted to do. Probably more times than you can count, right?

> **I cannot give you the formula for success, but I can give you the formula for failure - which is: try to please everybody.**
>
> **- Herbert B Swope**

Generally speaking, it is viewed as an incredibly noble gesture to put others ahead of yourself. And it is. Giving is a wonderful thing when you are in the place to give. The best place to exercise giving isn't necessarily when you are a billionaire, or you have everything you want either. Giving is *always* a good thing when the conditions don't come at the expense of *you:* your boundaries, your values and your health!

To best describe healthy giving, I always like to think of the safety procedures announcement after first boarding an airplane. In the event of a crash, oxygen masks will be deployed. It will always advise you to *put your own mask on first,* before assisting children and others. Although this is a simple example, essentially it does involve saying no to everyone else around you and taking care of your own needs first, so you are then in the best position to give assistance.

Every game changer in their relevant industry has learned the superpower of no, and uses it to their benefit. So it's time for you to rediscover the importance of saying no to anything that does not work in harmony with your **3W.** It is about remembering how to say no, similar to when you did when you were a child. No without guilt, shame and fear of the consequences. It's about unlearning the habit that you will not be loved if you say no to something; because that old people pleasing habit is so detrimental to your wellbeing and personal growth! It's about exercising your power to say no because of the bigger yes inside of you, and feeling confident and happy with your decision. This will be easy to do if you are diligent with your exercises in self worth! It's about doing what you need to do to set and maintain strong boundaries (uncomfortable as it might be at times), to live as your best and healthiest self. Once you are crystal clear and specific about what you ultimately want, it's a lot easier to know what to say no to.

Saying Yes To Everything is OverRated

Uh-oh, I can already sense the Positivity Paul's and Pollyanna's starting to protest. But you read that right. If you don't agree, could this be because you hold a belief that saying no is a negative thing, whine fact it's one of the most positive acts of self care that you can do for yourself?

There are many books and ideas out there that teach about the power of saying yes. Yes to all experiences! And yes, yes, *yes.* I get it. I'm all for grabbing life by the horns. I'm all for the hell yes when you're standing on the cliff wondering whether to **jump.**

But saying yes is a great thing when you are saying *yes with intention.* Saying yes with intention means saying yes to something because it is harmonious to all the factors that make up **The Mind Diet** program you've set for yourself. When you are saying yes with intention, it will also mean you are making the choice to say no to so many other choices out there. Because for every yes with intention executed, there is a multitude of no's that need to take place too! Blindly saying yes to everything for the sake of it is your express ticket to everywhere and nowhere all at once, and unfortunately, often where many of us find ourselves today.

> **People think focus means saying yes to the thing you've got to focus on. But that's not what it means at all. It means saying no to**

the hundred other good ideas that there are. You have to pick carefully. I'm actually as proud of the things we haven't done as the things I have done. Innovation is saying no to 1,000 things.

- Steve Jobs

Simplify and Just Say No.

Do you feel like you are burning the candle at both ends? Working all of the time without anything left for exercise? Rushing to drop off one child from football practice, to pick up the other one to go to dance class, to rush home to cook dinner? Are you overcommitted, and exhausting yourself in the process? Do you find yourself saying yes to please others, remain agreeable, and not rock the boat too much - even if it hurts your health, progress or greater goals? The solution is here!

It's time to innovate your life. And it starts with you and your courage to just say no. Rediscovering your right to say no is your **jump** to create the focus, intention and direction you need to reach your **Fitness Utopia**. Exercising your power of no (in line with your **whats, whys,** and **whens**), ensures the fastest route to your destination, while still being happy along the way. And who doesn't want that?

One of the most common barriers to exercise (and committing to a regular health plan) is that old, "I have no time to exercise or eat right" excuse. But we've all got time. We make time for the important things we feel we deserve. As they say, we've all got the same 24 hours a day as Beyonce. We choose where our time goes.

Take a look at your calendar. If you're seeing things in there that are not contributing to the greater good of your health and wellbeing, then do yourself a favor. Start to say no. You know what I mean. Those lunches. Those coffee meets. Those meetings, *and* those group texts. Simplify. Prioritize. Delegate. Delete. **You definitely have an hour a day to workout,** whether you get up earlier, or go to bed one hour later. It's in there if you are honest with yourself - but like all of these things, if you want to see the truth, you gotta be brave enough to look! To look honestly is to take responsibility, and make the changes necessary. This is your life, people! Drink that double shot of honesty serum, and have the courage to accept what you see for what it is.

I know we touched on self worth before, but it's worth mentioning again. You are so valuable! So is your energy, your time, and of course your health. They are your most valuable assets. So if you are using them to do things that do not make you better, then #DuhBecky, you have no business doing them. #JustSayNo

> **So what did I do? I started to say 'no'. I'm not taking that picture. I'm not going to that event. I'm not standing by that because that's not what I stand for. And slowly but surely, I remembered who I am. Then you go home and you look in the mirror and you're like, 'Yes, I can go to bed with you every night. 'Cause that person? I know that person. That person has balls. That person has integrity. That person just doesn't say yes.**
>
> **- Lady Gaga**

List some examples in the past where you were given the choice to say no but didn't, and regretted it later. This can be either health or non health related.

ACTUAL EVENT	ACTUAL DECISION	WHY I MADE THAT DECISION	WHAT I WOULD DO TODAY INSTEAD

This is a good exercise to complete, because what you may discover is you are reacting from your subconscious mind, and a 'people pleasing habit'. Bringing this into your conscious awareness can assist you in making a different decision next time. We forget so often in life that we have the power to choose. It is our greatest gift! Free will is a wonderful thing.

It gives you the ability to design and create your reality however you see fit.

Any person at the top of their field is aware of this superpower, and has created a habit to make good choices - and bad ones too, actually! The simple act of making a decision (with commitment and decisiveness), is an attribute that most winners possess, whether it's a winning choice or a choice that needs to be changed later. Like instilling any new habit, a conscious effort needs to be continually made to think of your **3W,** exercising due diligence with the appropriate exercises in **The Mind Diet,** and also learning to be okay with the uncomfortableness of saying no till it becomes a habit. With a little faith and consistency, you can go home knowing you have integrity, and knowing you're doing things in your life that are in line with what *you* stand for.

Step 7a: Say No and Let Go

What are a few things that you need to say no to? List below and also log *when* you are going to implement this, and add it to your schedule. An example might be you are not going to be able to give your work colleague a ride home every night, as you have decided that is the best time for you to go to the gym.

	SAYING NO SETTING A HEALTHY BOUNDARY	WHEN	
1			
2			
3			

	SAYING NO SETTING A HEALTHY BOUNDARY	WHEN	

The Mind Diet Mental Moves

EXERCISING THE POWER OF NO AND HEALTHY BOUNDARIES

If you're having difficulty feeling good about saying no, or setting healthy boundaries for yourself and are feeling stuck, here are some helpful exercises you can do below. Additionally, referring back to the exercises in *self worth* and *letting go* are also worthy endeavors that can prove beneficial over time.

Higher Self Talk

Talk to the person's higher self and ask for their compassion and understanding for setting this boundary.

Boundary Sand Bags

Write or endow each bag with the qualities of your best self. Hoist them up onto your shoulders. You must pick up each one and take it a distance. I recommend 200 meters. Work it!

Rope Circle

Get a rope and use it to make a circle on the ground. Then, on separate pieces of paper, write down the specific things you need to say no to get you to your **Fitness Utopia**. Place them in the circle.

Then, either write down on a piece of paper a description of your **Fitness Utopia** and how it makes you feel living as your best self. Really embody it! Alternatively, complete the Oscar Worthy Speech.

When you are ready, step into the circle as your best self. Pick up each piece of paper that is hindering your progress. Say, "I am worthy of health and I am worthy of love, so I choose to stand here and say no." Then throw it out of the circle. Repeat as necessary.

Variation on the Rope Circle (1)

This is a great group exercise. Everyone stands in a big circle with the subject in the middle. Instead of using a piece of paper, endow a tennis ball or beach ball with each entity you need to say no to outside of the circle. Describe it aloud, and throw it to any person standing in the bigger circle.

Take a few moments to step into the rope circle you've created. Stand in the circle as your best self. Close your eyes, and embody this first. Perhaps describe aloud who you are to the group using The Oscar Worthy Speech. Then, when you open your eyes, the balls are thrown at you. Each time it's thrown at you, you catch it. Think of what you have endowed the ball with and then repeat the mantra:

"I am worthy of health and I am worthy of love, so I choose to stand here and say no." Then, throw it back.

Variation on the Rope Circle (2)

This exercise is exactly as it's listed in the first variation, but instead of standing in the smaller rope you are simply standing in the bigger circle as your best self. Describe it aloud to the others to really embody it! When you open your eyes, balls are pegged at you and you have to dodge them, dodgeball style! Be prepared to move and sweat! See how fun fitness can be?!

The Lesson

The power of no is truly a wonderful gift and it's available to all of us. It is the ideal steering wheel and when used appropriately, ensures the most direct path to longterm fitness, health and happiness. When you commit to saying no to anything that doesn't work in line with your goals in **The Mind Diet**, you are actually saying yes to your health, and to your best self. So, don't say yes when you need to say no!

Chapter 10

Let Go Or Be Dragged.

What do you need to let go of to allow your results to catch you?

Today, one of my single girlfriends told me about an important decision she had made regarding her life. The decision was she wasn't going to have any old dick anymore. Inspiring, I know. She was not referring to old dick, in the traditional terms of age. She was referring to people she had dated previously and was going back to for a multitude of reasons: familiarity, boredom, drunken habits, etc. But from this day onwards, all old dick was off limits.

I found myself fist pumping the air, congratulating her. I actually thought it was quite courageous and progressive. Yes I get it, we're talking about casual dating, so how serious can it be? It's all fun and games when you're single, especially where we live in Los Angeles. I'm sure we can all remember a time when we went back to 'someone' or 'something', because it's just what we've done, or what we do. It's the old habit monster rearing it's head again and (as we know), old habits die hard.

But eventually, there comes a time (especially in relationships) where the 'situation-ship' dies, and casual sex just doesn't cut it anymore. My friend made this statement in a commitment to instill a new habit in her life. I'm sure she would like to meet someone who means more to her than anyone currently in her, ahem, *'dick-tionary,'* shall we call it? Her choice to stop seeing old dick is on her behalf, a **jump** to clear her head. To create the space for new dick, or dick that is more in line with her end goal of real love (with dick included obviously). #winning

It's not only in our relationships that we need to clear the old out before the new can come in. It's in our health and fitness too. Although I have written at length about the importance of letting go of your own individual toxic habits (and replacing them with new ones), it's not just in your own habits that this deep cleanse needs to occur. It's in your **entire environment!** The world as you see it through your eyes and your perception. Where you live, who you talk to, where you work, what you see, and what your surroundings are most of the time.

Fitness Mediocrity Land

Birds of the same feather fly together.

So lets imagine you are back out there, standing on the mountains edge, contemplating your first **jump** to the metal beam. But there are lots of people around you who are telling you not to **jump.**

They are not the people out there on the beam. They are standing on the ground next to you on the cliff, in *Fitness Mediocrity Land.* A land where being normal is the norm, and everyone fits into that ridiculous standardized bell curve that *Fitness Mediocrity Land* has created. There is a saying that misery loves company. Well, so does mediocrity, and really anything of the same feather.

> **They see me as a threat of some kind... I think every strong woman in history has had to walk down a similar path. It's the strength, that causes the confusion and the fear. Why is she strong? Where did she get it from? Where is she taking it? Where is she going to use it?**
>
> **- Princess Diana, Duchess of Wales**

While you surround yourself with the birds of *Fitness Mediocrity Land*, you are placing yourself in an environment that gives you permission and validation (and additionally all of the other mediocre birds permission and validation), to continue to be mediocre. Because that's what all the birds in *Fitness Mediocrity Land* do. Notice that the acronym for *Fitness Mediocrity Land* is FML. (That's why they pay me the big bucks, folks.)

Other notable traits of these birds are:

- Never flying even though they have wings. This is because it's too dangerous, and there is a legitimate risk of an accident.
- They each have individual reasons as to why they don't use their wings: they don't have time, they need to look after their chicks, or they are too old, etc. This is despite having perfectly functional and useable wings for flight.
- Habitually keeping their feet planted solidly, stubbornly and even proudly on the ground. They do this even though they are in fact better at flying than walking, and the ground is irritating on their feet.
- They exhibit toxic behavior to anyone who contemplates a jump, such as contempt, worry, jealousy, sadness, guilt, gossip, manipulation, or anger.
- All have had nagging dreams about the amazing views that may exist way out there (on the metal beam) past the **jump**.

Any initial decision to jump from *Fitness Mediocrity Land* will not be met favorably. This is because this mediocre crew will lose some of it's company. Changes in numbers to the flock make everyone nervous. It's always safer in larger numbers. Additionally, every contemplation to **jump** from a rogue bird reminds everyone of their own lost **jumps** (even though some birds will never admit it). Each bird that actually **jumps** removes some validation from the flock that it's OK for birds to live on the ground. They spend their days on the ground together, gossiping about those unusual, crazy, rogue jumpers. I mean, who do those birds think they are?

Toxic Entities

Everyone pushes a falling fence.
- Chinese Proverb

You see, now that you are clearly aware of **what** you want, and **why** you want these things, it becomes very easy to spot anything that does not work in line with these parameters. They stick out like sore thumbs. The shocking thing is, many of the factors that do not work in line with your **3W** could have been entities that have been in your world for months, years - or even your entire lifetime! When you really stop and think about it, how could your **3W** have been achieved in a space that was so uncomplimentary for it to occur?

In addition to your own habits, this is one of the biggest

determining factors in the achievement (or the non achievement) of your health goals, and indeed any goal you'd like to achieve in life. It's a game-changer folks: Whether you launch and fly to the beam, or you stay put on the ground!

The entities I am referring to can include:

- A toxic place you frequent, such as a bar, pub, a person's house, or even your own home.
- Your significant other's drinking and partying habits.
- A ritual. For example, every birthday in your workplace means everyone goes out somewhere and gets shit-faced. It's an unofficial company rule.
- A family member or your entire family not caring about nutrition or health at all.
- A group of friends or friend that hates the gym and think people who exercise are self indulgent.
- A self limiting, toxic belief e.g. you have no time to exercise, or you can't afford to exercise.
- A toxic entity you are addicted to: cigarettes, alcohol, drugs, or food.
- Your own toxic habits such as self sabotage, or always running late.

Therapy has allowed me to discover that my childhood was an environment where there was no real sense of boundaries instilled regarding people that came into my space and my life. Did I mention my mother is Fijian? The culture is known for its communal living, and my family home was always filled with people. Coming home on any given day, you never knew who you were going to meet there. In therapy, and in exploring the topics of self love and self worth (which I will delve into later on), I discovered the utmost importance of establishing healthy boundaries for myself *at all times.* My mother (to this day), still puts up with a lot of individuals that many others would have left the hell alone. Individuals that do not play well with others. While that's another story altogether, I always grew up thinking that I just needed to put up with people as they were. And obviously, there are a lot of special personalities on planet Earth. That's what makes this place such an adventure. As Forrest Gump said, "Life's like a box of chocolates, you never know what you're gonna get!"

And my mother is right. People are the way they are, and try as we might, we cannot change anyone. If anyone has tried to tell you to change your behavior, (or certain things about yourself before), you probably have only done it if you have been committed to the change, and **you** have wanted to do it. This is because (again), we are dealing with our habits. As we know, changing them is a bitch to do.

But while it's true that you cannot change people, you definitely can **choose the people and situations** you are around. Perhaps it seems like an elementary discovery for many of you. "Duh Edwina," I hear you mutter. But is it? How many times have you let people, situations, and places take up space in your mind, heart and life - when it has come at the expense of your peace, respect, health, and happiness? How many times are you reacting to your environment, instead of making conscious and healthy choices to create a reality that is congruent with a harmonious journey to your **what/s?** My hunch is that if there weren't some toxic entities in your current environment right now, you wouldn't be reading this book, and you'd be sipping on sugar free cocktails by the pool in your **Fitness Utopia.**

In order to create the reality (and everything that you have dreamt your **Fitness Utopia** to be), you must first **create the space** for the magic to occur. This means taking responsibility for everything that has happened in your life thus far; that has shaped it the way we see it at this very moment. It means having the courage to let go, or **strongly redefine** the role (and importance) of those toxic entities, and anything that stands in your way of getting there - even if it's all you've ever known. Wakey wakey, hands off snakey! Life is happening, folks! Once you realize how powerful you are, and that you can create your reality **exactly** as you have envisioned it, the fun can truly begin. Finally, you are awake! You're in the drivers seat, and the world is your oyster. You get to decide **where** you're going, **who** and **what** is coming along, **how** you are going to get there, **how fast** you are going to go, and **when** you are going to arrive. It's up to you. It's always been up to you!

The Mass Exodus.

I want to talk with you about a period of my life that I refer to as **The Mass Exodus**. It was in the wake of the worst breakup of my entire lifetime. Today, I can stand before you, and share honestly it has taken me nearly three years to genuinely understand and appreciate the lessons of that relationship, and realize it was the **best thing** to have ever happened to me for my own growth and transformation.

Because in order to step into my greatness, and in order to know my worth, I needed to have someone emotionally drain me in a manner that was so destructive and unhealthy, that I had *no choice* but to either commit soul suicide and perish as the woman I was, or to stand up and fight for myself, and put up the boundaries that I so desperately needed there. In the wake of that breakup, I began to go to therapy regularly. Over time, I learned the value in having healthy boundaries. I learned I was worth so much more than I ever imagined. I learned about the importance of self care, and self love.

> **You don't ever have to feel guilty about removing toxic people from your life. It doesn't matter whether someone is a relative, romantic interest, employer, childhood friend or new acquaintance. You don't have to make room for people who cause you pain or make you feel small. It's one thing if a person owns up to their behavior and makes an effort to change. But if a person disregards your feelings, ignores your boundaries, and "continues"**

to treat you in a harmful way, they have to go.
— Danielle Koepke

With the guidance of my therapist, I installed some rickety ass boundaries. At the time, if someone was to see a literal creation of my boundaries, I imagine it would have looked like old pieces of plastic and newspaper haphazardly stapled together in some weird fashion. It was scary, because for the first time in my life I started to really say **no.** I began to see how beneficial this was for my health, wellbeing and happiness. And with these rickety boundaries installed, I began to notice some very alarming things. And this was the glaring realization that my life was full of entities that did not fit within these new healthy parameters. To be honest, nearly all of it was.

So, with these new discoveries (and my boundaries in mind), **The Mass Exodus** began. No situation, and no person was spared. No matter the time I had known them, past history and experiences, working situations… *nothing.* If an entity brought toxicity in any manner into my space, they had to go.

Because for the first time in my life, I believed in my heart I was worth it. And I knew I would never be able to be all I was meant to be, if I continued to ignore the healthy boundaries that I had installed (rickety as they were). I knew I needed to create the space for new energy to enter so my health, happiness and life could flourish the way I envisioned it.

Just when the caterpillar thought the world was over, she became a butterfly.
– Barbara Haines Howett

When you are at your best and healthiest self, you are then in a position to be able to help others be the best they can be. If you have guilt (or shame) about treating yourself with respect, and feel bad for taking measures to create an environment for you to live in a healthy, peaceful manner, then it's time to let that go. **Right now.**

It's pure insanity to set yourself on fire to make others feel warm. You'll burn yourself in the process, and then all of you are up shit creek. By the same token, there is no nobility in destroying yourself for the sake of another entity. It is the highest act of self care, and self love to protect yourself from those around you that are stopping you from stepping into your greatness in health, wellness, and any journey to greatness you are making in this lifetime.

Step 7b: Say No and Let Go

Now that you have very clear goals with clear deadlines, stop and think about the entities in your life that hinder your progress to being the best you can be. What relationships do you then need to **redefine** or **let go** of to allow your results to catch you? List them below. Then, decide on what **jump** or action you can schedule right now to create the safe, healthy space for your **Fitness Utopia** to become a reality.

TOXIC ENTITY	ACTION	WHEN

Often, if the toxic entities are significant others (or are family members), it may not be as easy to establish the boundaries you need, to protect yourself in the way it should. That still doesn't mean nothing is to be done, though. You don't get off the hook that easily, folks! Your health is too important to live another moment in *Fitness Mediocrity Land!*

If having direct conversations with them does not illicit an understanding of your boundaries, I would suggest hiring a marriage or family therapist (or a relevant professional), that can coach and mediate through these types of relationships, so a common, cheerful ground can be reached.

You gotta know when to hold em, and know when to fold em.
- Kenny Rogers

Perhaps you've noticed that many of the entities that take up space in your life today are toxic to your health and wellbeing. It can be sad, (and scary) to realize that this is all you've ever known. If those entities are not there, what will be in place of them? Your **Fitness Utopia**, and the cheerful entities that compliment it! It's about flexing your **faith muscle up** so you'll begin to take the **jumps** necessary to say goodbye to those entities as you know them at this moment.

If you're freaking out, looking at your list and thinking this will mean a complete overhaul of your life, rest assured that many others are with you on this path. You never walk alone, even though sometimes it might feel like it. Additionally, this is why it is paramount to have a good grasp of your **3W.** Referring to your **why** should be strong enough to immediately contemplate the **jumps** required to create the space for your **what** to manifest. Knowing your **when** is very effective in providing a sense of urgency. Because as we know, (for the majority of us), if there ain't a fire under our butts, we ain't doing much!

They say don't believe your own hype, but if you don't why would anyone else? To be great you have to believe you can do great things.

- Charley Johnson

Yo. You Got This!

It can be scary to stand up and step out alone. To make a leap of faith and **jump**, when often all you've known is life on the ground. To be a flamingo in a sea of pigeons. To believe in your heart that you are worth more than what your health, and wellbeing might be at this moment in time.

But rest easy knowing that out there on the beam, there is another crew. A new crew, in line with your journey to your **Fitness Utopia.** Let's call them *The Flight Crew.*

Just like the crew on the ground of the cliff, they also *love* company. *The Flight Crew* always want you to **jump,** because what's better than flying high in health with those in your life that are special to you? They encourage. They call out joyfully to you from the beam to **jump**. They may even throw you some bird seeds to give you a little energy push. Take it, because I'll bet someone once threw them seeds.

Then you have a choice: You can decide whether to use this energy to gossip with all of the other birds in *Fitness Mediocrity*

Land, or fuel yourself to focus on mapping out your own journey and preparing for your own **jumps**. And feel excited that one day you'll pay it forward, and throw your own seeds to help others across. But that's *only* if you choose to make that first **jump!**

Shadow work is the path of the heart warrior.
- Carl Jung

There is a saying that we can never rise up to heaven, unless our roots have gone down into hell. And just like my breakup, it was through experiencing a complete disregard for my space, my dreams, my sense of self worth and my safety from a person that I loved - that forced me to grow into the person I am today. To find the courage to stand up for myself, say enough is enough, and install the healthy boundaries I so desperately needed. To create the habit to let go of toxic entities, and create a space for cheerful and joyful things to grow in their place. To feel a sense of worth so highly, that I live my life in my **Fitness Utopia,** without shame or guilt in doing so. To practice self care so diligently, that I have let go of people you wouldn't believe even if I told you.

Multimillionaires, celebrities, professional athletes, people I've grown up with, ex-boyfriends, fuck-boys, toxic friends. *The Mass Exodus* was a life cleanse of the most extreme kind.

I don't mention *The Mass Exodus* as some kind of boast, or out of maliciousness. Today, it's all love and elevation over here. I mention this to make you aware that soon (if you haven't already), some hard decisions will need to be made for the greater good of your health and happiness. I also mention it because I'm so freaking proud of the person I've become. Because I fought so hard to become her! As weird as this sounds, it was *hard* to say no to toxicity. Because up until that point, that was all I knew of.

If you are one of the people that I no longer engage with, know this: my heart bleeds for you, and I hope reading this book will help you to rise the way **The Mind Diet** has helped me. At the end of the day, we are all just humans trying to make sense of it all, and for that I will always have love for you. But somewhere along the way, you'll understand it was never about hating you - I don't hate anyone! There's no space in the reality I've created for hate, negativity or disrespect. That's what I was jumping away from in the first place! But it was about loving me. It was about self care and protection. It was about deciding exactly **what** I wanted, **why** I wanted it (and through these exercises that I'll share below), it was about rising to the belief that I was worth all of these things and more. It was about taking courageous **jumps** of self care in the highest regard. It was about stepping into my greatness and my worth, so I could then be in the place to create and share my gifts with the world - which include writing this book! It was about reporting for duty for my life's mission: to pass on these tools to help **you** (the reader), become everything you were supposed to be in health, fitness, and in life.

If you don't love your selfie, how in the hell you gonna love anybody else-ie?
- Ru Paul

Take a look at the numerous exercises I've listed below, and choose those that resonate with you. Not all will work, but many will. Explore and discover what makes you tick, by capitalizing on your own personal triggers to create consistent healthy habits. Exercises that will aid you in permanently letting go (or redefining your relationship) with those toxic entities, and creating the space that you need for your goals to come into fruition.

You are worth so much more than you may realize! Everything is gonna be fantastic, just as soon as you're ready to make it so.

Note: Before you begin these exercises, I urge you to stay open to the possibility of transformation. What you were doing previously hasn't worked, or hasn't worked to the level you wished it had, right? The people who live in their **Fitness Utopia** first believed that it could happen to them.

So take a chance, and believe it can be true for you too. And why not you? If everyone else… why not you too?
#YouAreWorthy

The Mind Diet Mental Moves

On Exercises in Self Worth

As well as your environment, one of the main reasons you do not possess the health you desire is due to a self limiting belief (along with supporting habits that cause you to believe) that you don't deserve this health, *or are not deserving enough of it* to make the changes necessary.

Armed with your **3W, The Mind Diet** is also about exploring the topic of your self worth, and doing appropriate exercises in self care to create the environment for health to manifest.

Here are some of my favorites below.

Your Journal of Worth

Buy a journal or calendar, preferably a bright one. Every morning, look into the mirror and write down three things you like about yourself. It can be anything. **Do this everyday.** Take pride in this journal, and write with colored markers! Write with intention. Over time, you'll start to see what a great person you are, and what amazing gifts you bring to the world that only you have. Flip through it regularly for that extra boost!

Worthy Indulgences

At least once every week, schedule an indulgence that makes you feel good. Is it a massage, a nail appointment, or a rental of your favorite luxury car? Schedule something that you enjoy and tell yourself everyday, *you are worthy* of this enjoyment that you have scheduled because you are **you**.

If you are finding it difficult to release the guilt of having these appointments, do something nice for someone that doesn't expect it. It can be something small, such buying a coffee for someone, paying someone's car ticket, sending flowers, or a card letting someone know you appreciate them and everything they do. Smile and receive all the good vibes that come with doing things for people. How do you feel now?

Oprah Interview

It is my biggest dream for this book not only to be a NY Times Bestseller, but for me to be on Oprah talking about it, and how it can help so many people step into their greatness in health, and in their lives. You can do the same too, with your transformation and your journey to your **Fitness Utopia.** Imagine you have arrived - what do you look like and how do you feel? Now walk out onto The Oprah Show and talk to her about how you did it.

Positivity Jam

This is also listed earlier but it's great for creating joy! With technology at our fingertips, it's so easy to have it with you at all times. Play in the car and listen to it and dance like no one is watching. They might be, but who cares if you're happy?

Oscar Worthy Speech

Visualize you have reached your goal utopia and you are standing in front of your **why** (or a crowd of people). Talk to them about how you found your power to achieve your goals. Speak of discovering your worth and how it helped you step into your greatness. If you don't feel worthy, think about someone who possesses those worthy qualities and talk as if you have them. (Which you do!)

Oscar Worthy Speech (Active Variation)

Start this exercise like you are going to start a 100 meter dash. Endow the finish line with your **Fitness Utopia**. Sprint to the finish line, then begin you Oscar Worthy Speech knowing you have reached your goal.

The Worthy Giver

Give. Volunteer your time, your money, or decide on something that you can do to help someone else. We touched on this in the previous exercise, but it's worth mentioning again: Nothing raises your feel good frequency than doing something for someone that doesn't expect it! And if you believe what goes around comes around, any actions of giving are going to be returned to you tenfold. So give, and know you are special and worth so much for doing so.

Worthy Passions

Begin a new hobby by doing something you have always wanted to do, but had previously been left in the 'Someday Pile for Someday'. As we are referring to health and fitness, decide on something that is active and that will get you out and moving. P.S. If you have decided this hobby is Pokemon Go, for goodness sake be careful!

I know I had mentioned previously that Someday was not listed in the calendar. I'm sorry, but I'm mistaken. It *is* in the calendar. Someday is TODAY! **Today is your day** to find (or rediscover) your passion for fitness, and for life. Often, feelings of low self worth is due to a feeling of loss in overall purpose. If you are in this position, **action** is key. Get out there and start trying different things, exploring new environments and discover what you're good at. Everyone is good at something, you just need to find out what that is for you. Being good at something and doing that 'thing' often can work wonders on raising self worth and happiness. Your talents have a tendency to lead you to your passion. I know it did for me. So stay curious, and don't give up! It's there.

Tell Me More

This is a great exercise for groups (either for work colleagues or family members). Each person takes a turn at being the subject. The rest of the group speaks about things they love about them and their positive attributes.

Tell Me More (Active Variation)

Set a time limit (about 1-2 minutes). One person grabs a sandbag (or ball) with a quality that another person likes about them. The person tells them what it is, in a simple way. Such as, "I love your sensitivity". The person grabs the sensitivity ball, says thank you then either races to another marker and drop it there, or can even shoot it through a basketball hoop. They need to try and get as many balls/bags to the other side or through the hoop.

Hot Box of Applause

Another great group exercise is to have a person enter the room. As they enter the room, everyone stands and starts cheering and clapping for that one person for an entire minute. The more people, the better. The louder the better. The crazier the better! I'm talking wolf cries, whistles, beating on anything you can find, hollering, hooting, shrieking, uncivilized madness. This exercise is a winner!

If you have any of your own that you love, and would like to share, I always love hearing about them. Tweet me! @eddsthetics

The Mind Diet Mental Moves

Exercises in Letting Go

If you let go a little, you will have a little peace. If you let go a lot, you will have a lot of peace.
- Ajahn Chah

Every moment is your chance to make a choice to let go of what isn't serving your greater good to health and your right to feel peace. Here are some of my top exercises in letting go.

Power To Choose

Consider the entity in question. Observe any emotions that come up and fully choose to welcome those feelings. Choose to completely let them in, no matter what they are.

Now think, if I chose to let those emotions completely in, can I choose to let those emotions go? Are you willing to let those emotions go?

If the answer is yes, when are you going to choose to do it? Now? If the answer is no, what do you gain by keeping this entity with you? If we are holding onto something we are gaining some benefit from it.

Perhaps in trying to let go of this entity, you have discovered a self limiting belief that you have had for a long time that is making it difficult. Perhaps letting go of it will mean taking responsibility for your life. Perhaps it will mean admitting you are wrong about the story you have told yourself and the association that comes with it. Perhaps, upon exploring, there are other self limiting beliefs or fundamental entities that you also need to let go of before redefining the story that you initially started this exercise with.

For example: I still remember the time when I first tried a banana as a kid. I ate one, and happened to suffer from a migraine shortly after. For years, just the smell of banana conjured feelings of weakness, a throbbing sensation in my head, and loss of sight and feeling on half of my body.

I decided I hated bananas, and wouldn't even go near them, behaving like I had some kind of allergy. In time, I discovered from my orthodontist that the reason for my migraines was to do with my teeth and the alignment of my jaw. Subsequently, having braces fixed my migraines forever. But even after braces, I still did not eat bananas! By this time, I had also forgotten why I didn't eat them (as it was now part of my subconscious habits). It was only after doing many of the exercises in this book and uncovering many of my now unconscious habits and decisions that I was able to realize the falseness of this claim. That bananas are awesome. I chose to write a new story. Now I eat bananas all of the time!

Repeat this process as often as needed, either by yourself or with emotional support. Do this until you feel free of the particular feeling you began with - or until you feel relaxed, open, lighter, confident, and at ease.

The Chair Dump

I learned this exercise from a spiritual thinker called Adyashanti. All you need are two chairs.

Sit in one chair, and think about the entity that you are having a problem with. Feel it deeply. Think about the overall emotion that you are experiencing. Is it anger? Fear? Sadness?

Now, think about who, from your childhood most embodies this situation. Stay with the association and feel whatever comes up. Note: You are not blaming them, simply associating this feeling and emotion with them. This should take about two minutes or so.

When you are ready, get up and leave the old energy (and the weight of this) behind in the first chair with that association. Sit down in the other chair.

Feel the lightness of leaving that entity behind.

Cutting Ties

This exercise was one of the most cathartic and useful exercises I had during the time of *The Mass Exodus.* Cutting Ties is a great activity for setting healthy boundaries up with entities that exist in your life that, whether they realize or not, are taking up space in your life that come at the expense of your greater health and greater good. When deploying Cutting Ties properly, it is incredibly successful in cutting toxic, (yet cosmic) connections that seem unbreakable and unseen to the naked eye. If you've ever gone through a breakup and many months pass yet you still find yourself in the same place, stuck and unable to move on, you'll know what I am talking about. Its presence and connection lingers like a bad smell, almost as if you are both still tuned into the same frequency. Because you are!

1. Find a quiet place, close your eyes and spend a few moments centering yourself.

2. Keeping your eyes closed, visualize that the entity in question is across from you. Note that this entity may or

may not be a person, and can be any of the toxic entities I had mentioned at the start of this chapter (or one of your own additional examples.) Imagine you are seeing the cosmic ties that bind you and this toxic entity together. What do the ties look like? How big, what color and how many are there? Where are they connecting to and from on your body (and theirs)? How does this make you feel?

3. When you are ready, say thank you to this toxic entity for it's lessons in self care and self love. Talk to them for the last time. Forgive them, forgive yourself, then start to cut the ties. What are you cutting them with? How many do you need to cut? How does this make you feel? After the ties have been cut, say goodbye, then walk away.

4. When you are ready, open your eyes. How do you feel? Journal if it feels cathartic. And just like most of these exercises in **The Mind Diet**, how many times this exercise is scheduled into your workout and completed for it to be a success is based largely on your own individual situation, commitment, consistency and willingness to let go. If you start to feel the energy of that toxic entity and it's ties around you, simply remind yourself of when you cut these

ties. Say no & let go, so you can finally move forward.

The Balloon Drop

I had listed The Balloon Drop as an option to build good habits in Chapter 7. Additionally, The Balloon Drop can be useful in letting go of toxic entities outside of yourself, such as other people.

1. Write each of your unhealthy habits/toxic entities on each balloon. You can also grab your workout buddies and do it together. This is a fun, cathartic group exercise!

2. In a circle, each person takes their turn standing in the middle and talking of how each particular endowed balloon has stopped them from stepping into your best self in health and/or life. Dwell on the weight of what each balloon represents. If you are doing this exercise alone, I find it better to speak out aloud as if people were there.

3. When you are ready to let go of each balloon, repeat this sentence: "Today, *I choose* to release the need for this in my

life."

4. Then let go and release. Feels good, doesn't it?

Heavy Load

1. Grab a backpack and fill it with tennis balls.

2. Imagine the tennis balls represent the specific entities you would like to redefine your relationship with.

3. Start running and don't stop. While you are running dwell on the weight of these balls and how heavy your backpack has become. Without blame, associate the weight with your toxic entity.

4. Run until you can't run anymore. When you are ready to let go, stop and say, "*I choose* to release the need to have this in my life."

5. Either throw each ball as far away as you can from you. Literally peg it. Or empty the bag of tennis balls into a trash

bag. Label it as your toxic entity… then take it to donate to the GoodWill bin, to the neighborhood tennis court, to an animal shelter, to a school - the list is endless. Someone else has good use for all of your balls. But you do not need them any longer!

The Mind Diet Schedule

I cannot stress the importance of scheduling these exercises into your calendar with as much regularity as your workouts and your meal plan. Refer back to Becky's schedule in Chapter 3 if you need a good example of how to program your **Mind Diet Mental Moves.**

If you are still doubtful on the power of these exercises over time, consider this:

Any individual that has reached their **Fitness Utopia** learns that they have achieved this mastery by committing to the details. They found their strength in the specifics. Complete one workout with 100% intensity and commitment, and sure, you may go home that day, and look in the mirror and see no noticeable change. But do this workout everyday with 100% intensity and commitment, and it may surprise you how fast you progress. Combining your exercise plan with **The Mind Diet** will give you the specific tools to elevate your mental fitness game to create the space required for lasting physical changes to occur, and with a lot less chance of being derailed by toxic old habits and self sabotage.

If you're thinking, "Edwina, I've never been consistent with my health and fitness - that's why I'm reading this book!" Well, the key to unlocking lasting success in this arena begins with a commitment to doing these exercises. If you can't do the small stuff, how can you do the big stuff, right? So add them into your schedule like you would add a workout. Trust the process, and prepare for your life to transform.

There is a ridiculous phrase in fitness that says, "Fitness is x% exercise, and x% diet." I've heard many variations of the percentage split, from 80/20 to 20/80 to 100/100. Whilst the latter makes no mathematical sense whatsoever, I'm going to use my own mathematical powers to redefine this phrase:

Fitness is:

100% Exercise

100% Nutrition

100% Mind Diet

Equals 300% of totally awesome bro!

Maybe it's not mathematically sound... But it still makes sense right?

The Lesson

No reason for something to stay, is a good reason for something to go.

Chapter 11

A Cheerful Space

In my years of working with others, I've learned that the human body is a miraculously malleable instrument that you should be proud to have, and excited to use and operate! One human body can be designed, modified and used in largely different ways. Even after all of this time, it still surprises and excites me how flexible it is, and how large a transformation can be with a little consistency and commitment. The possibilities are endless!

If you are doing the exercises as you read **The Mind Diet,** and you have executed letting go of many of the things you need to let go of, I want to give you a double high five through the cosmos. I'm squealing in the corner like a stage Mom watching her kid's first dance recital. I imagine you are perhaps standing in your Rope Circle alone, because many of the things that shaped your identity previously are not within your boundary line anymore, and you've let them go. From the bottom of my heart, I'm so mother hen proud of you!

It's scary to stand up for yourself. Often it means standing alone. But exercise your **faith muscle up,** armed with the knowledge that this is part of the process - and just hold on! We all go through it in some way, whether it was as extreme as *The Mass Exodus* I experienced, or whether you've committed to simply taking the time to mentally redefine the importance (and role) of those entities in question; so you can create a healthy space for you to make your **Fitness Utopia** a reality.

So here you are. A blank page. New boundaries, and healthy habits have been instilled, with a commitment to follow through. What's next?

A Pledge to Higher Standards

Not every place you fit in is where you belong.

One of my favorite books is called, *The Life-Changing Magic of Tidying Up,* by Marie Kondo. If you haven't read it, I highly recommend it. The book is about how to organize and get rid of the clutter in your home. The general premise is this: if you pick up any item that's in your home and it doesn't bring you joy, then you need to get rid of it. Overall, it's a great strategy for tidying things up, and a neat way for you to simplify and decide what's really important to you.

I always have this concept with me as I go about my everyday life, but of course with my own flavor added to it. And that is the concept of only adding cheer - or cheerful things into my space. I think of it when standing on my own mountain's edge, and I'm about to make a decision. And you should too! Because here you are, the designer of your life. You can choose to fill it with what you like. Why not choose to fill it with things that *only* bring you cheer, and all of the cheerful, joyful entities that support you living your life as your healthiest, most cheerful and greatest self?

Here is my invitation to you. Pledge to yourself to create a life of cheer, and join all of us out here on the beam that have made the jump to it. Because you are not alone, you just need to fly with your kinda people. Eagles don't roll with pigeons, yo. Whatever type of life you accept and you believe you deserve, is **exactly** what you'll get. So choose to believe you deserve cheer. Choose to **jump** for cheer only, and watch the magic unfold!

On the next page, make it a priority to write "cheer" in the area below it. I've found it easiest to have a copy I've laminated that sits near my desk in my office. I update it daily with a whiteboard marker.

If this seems like an unreasonable standard for you, simply refer back to your exercises exploring self worth. The Chair Dump is also a good activity to consider adding into your schedule. It's a great tool for exploring and discovering who in your past has shaped your view that living with cheer all of the

TODAY

I CHOOSE

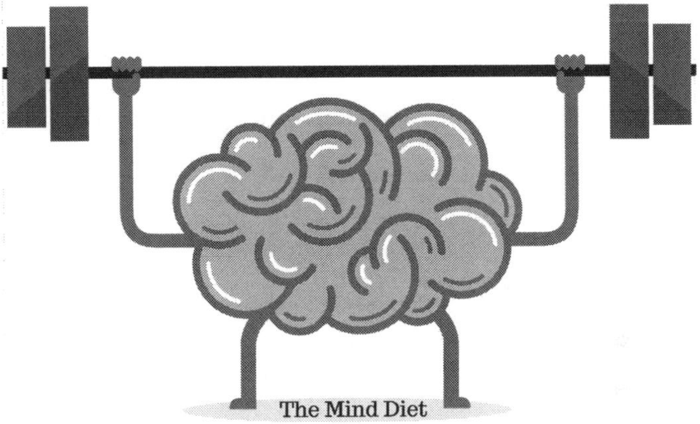

time is an unreasonable reality, and/or shaped the belief that you are not deserving of it, (or deserving enough) to have it in your life everyday. Without blame, simply associate that belief with them. Then let that stuff go and keep moving forward. Because your life of cheer awaits! Once you make a sincere commitment to a higher standard, it's even easier to know what to say no to, and to know what to welcome in.

Note: This means also pledging to a higher standard for yourself too. Which involves working to only choose to indulge cheerful thoughts. I get it, shit happens! And maybe it will get you down. You'll make mistakes, you'll fall off your exercise plan, or screw up on your nutrition. But you just gotta keep getting up. That's what it's all about. And when you have a life of cheerful things, and you're also working hard to fuel your **thoughts of cheer only,** it's very hard to stay down in those places. In time, those cheerful habits (and the cheerful surroundings that you've chosen), will pick you right back up to what you know, and the cheerful reality you've created.

So now that you are creating your space, choose the highest level of cheer that you can muster. Everyday! And choose cheerful people. If you've worked hard to create positive, cheerful vibes, cheerful people will naturally flock to you. The good thing about this is that it's like a big rolling snowball. You'll feed off each others 'cheers', and rise even higher together.

My Two Cents

There is definitely some great reasoning for keeping things on the down low from most of the world when you are first forging out into unchartered waters. This is because the change you have decided to make can feel like you are in a vulnerable position. **The Mind Diet** works to identify, uproot and change those toxic behaviors and beliefs that stop you from living your life in your **Fitness Utopia**. To contemplate the decision to **jump,** prepare to launch, and then create your cheerful space takes so much courage on your part. At this initial stage, your own mind and body may try and play tricks on you to push you to go back to how things were.

As well as that, you may be dealing with how others are reacting to your changes too, As we know, humans are very resistant to change. If you are just starting to create a new space, and you are still building your *Flight Crew*, you are at risk of having the wrong people enter, and project their own limits onto your dreams (based on their own experiences and life). You risk being swept back into the electromagnetic field of fear that exists around most of us today. Similar to a black hole, or a rip in the ocean, the pressure of it can be so intense; that if you get caught in it at this vulnerable stage, you may find yourself back at square one: in *Fitness Mediocrity Land*… or in fact, sometimes square zero, with that recent 'failure' taking root in adding validation to your fears - thereby solidifying its reality. And so the toxic cycle continues!

So, remember, at this point: **tolerance is overrated**. Don't allow yourself to fall back into those old toxic habits, and steer clear from the electromagnetic waves of toxic people that are reinforcing the old unhealthy habits you have been trying so hard to uproot and change. *I cannot stress this enough.* They will stop your progress dead in its tracks because that's their habit. And it was probably yours at one point too. So no judgements, no hate, but remember: you gotta do what's best for you. If you've worked hard to make changes for your own health and wellness (and your own greater good), you don't owe anyone the person you used to be. There's nothing wrong with growing and discovering your purpose or healthy mission and deciding to go after it. But as we talked about previously, defining your **3W**, and embarking on your journey may give you the awareness that in order to finish what you started, you will need to let some people out along the way.

In this life we are all fabulously worthy creatures traveling at our own pace. There is no shame in your individual pace, or anyone else's for that matter. Perhaps you have been left behind by others, and that's okay too. Not everyone is meant to stay, and many lessons may not have been learned if they were still there. So honor your place, open your eyes to your special, **individual** journey (and its lessons), and who knows: maybe you'll meet them on the flip side. This journey to health (or any other journey you take in life), is your own. We are against no one but ourselves. So honor your own pace, remember your worth, and no matter what - keep moving forward!

In the topic of relationships, perhaps only choosing a cheerful partner can be seen as too picky, unrealistic, or always looking for the next best thing. But I don't see it like that at all. For anyone who is in a happy, healthy marriage, I would argue they see cheer in their lives everyday. If you are not finding something to be cheerful about **every single day** in a relationship you are in, (whether it's romantic or platonic), then I'd argue that you gotta change your perspective to redefine this relationship as you see it to include cheer - or you gotta let it go. Life's too short to not have the most cheerful time possible while we are here! And why not, if it's available to you. #ChooseCheer

Step 8: Create Your Space Of Cheer

Let's go back to the examples you listed in the last chapter as the jumps you were going to take to exercise your power of no.

	SAYING NO SETTING A HEALTHY BOUNDARY	WHEN	JOYFUL REPLACEMENT
1	I will say no to drinking alcohol during the week when I am invited out, and say I have a spa appointment.	Effective Today	When I am asked, I say no and then book myself into the Wii Spa. It's only $20 and I can stay for a long as I want!
2			
3			

Building on this, what joyful jumps or action are you going to put in place, in line with your **3W**? I've given you an example of my own.

Additionally, what are three new things you can do to create or maintain your space of cheer in health and fitness?

Creating Cheer

1	
2	
3	

Update every Monday.

The Mind Diet Rewards System

I've always found it helpful to have little rewards scheduled along the way if I'm successful in reaching those **little d** milestones I had mapped out. This rewards system builds on the ideas of Chapter 3 and your little d's.

Ultimately, the best way to do it would be to add it into your schedule as a tentative booking, just after you have reached a *little d.* For example, let's say you have listed one of your **little d's** to have lost 1lbs. If you are successful in this, reward yourself with something cheerful. Schedule it soon afterwards, so we can build the habit of a positive and cheerful association with reaching your *little d's.*

It is also paramount that these cheerful things do not involve reversing your progress in health and wellness. In other words, do not make your reward a cheat day at McDonalds, or a boozy weekend in Vegas. It also doesn't have to be a big affair or expensive. What it does have to be is **cheerful/joyful to you.**

Some examples may include:

- A massage
- Catching a movie at the theater
- Nail salons
- A day at the beach relaxing
- An art gallery visit
- A concert or event of interest
- A purchase of something of cheer to you, such as a new music album, a sexy little black dress, a new pair of shoes you've had your eye on
- A course you've always wanted to do
- Buying a book you've wanted to read and taking the day off to read it
- The day off to hang out with your dog
- Taking a staycation with your significant other

Once you have these rewards scheduled after your **little d's,** the most important thing to do now is to **stick with it.** That means no rewards are to be taken if your **little what's** haven't been achieved in line with your **little d's.** If you are off track or behind schedule, you need to adjust these rewards in line with the adjustments you've made to your **little what's/ little d's.**

Additionally, it's a good idea to appoint an accountability partner, or make someone supportive aware of your path and plans. The right accountability partner can be a great asset to help motivate and keep you accountable to reach those milestones you've set.

The Lesson

#ChooseCheer. You are worth it!

Chapter 12

Run Your Own Race

Winners focus on winning.
Losers focus on winners.
Michael Phelps

These days, a few clicks of a button can connect you to anyone you want, anywhere in the world. I know what a girl I went to school with had for dinner last night, simply by logging onto Facebook. I haven't spoken in a conversation with her for over ten years though. Absurd, isn't it? Yet, I know her husband's name (that I've never met), and her kids and how old they are. I know she just got a promotion, and she has booked a trip to Mykonos next summer for two weeks. She's also lost fifteen pounds after her second child, and she's Vegan. And she swears by it.

I'm sure that you have many examples of your own that you can refer to. We are bombarded with information everyday about the lives and brands of other people. PR and social media firms are paid big dollars to present a brand or a person's highlight reel; so it shines brighter than any of the competition out there.

I think one of a good PR agency's best attributes is having an astute sense of *exactly how* to roll a piece of shit in glitter. You guys, I'm serious. If you can take a piece of poop, literally roll it around in glitter, knowing how much glitter to add, how many rolls in the glitter, the color of the glitter, and how to light it correctly in the most flattering way (that will result in a call to action from viewers) then brands, or people (or both), are paying you the big bucks. It's astounding what a good marketing campaign, a press release, and targeted advertising can do for a regular someone or something!

And we scroll through these campaigns, perfect pictures with ten filters on it and three rounds of photoshop. Glossy plates filled with perfectly positioned food, perfectly manicured houses and gardens, perfect bodies on the beach with perfect partners in perfect relationships. And we know, deep down… it's not real. By now, I believe we all know the difference between a raw image and a photoshopped one. But like addicted voyeurs, we keep scrolling, looking, judging, comparing ourselves… trying to keep up. We just can't help it!

But whenever we are busy watching, we aren't busy working on ourselves. Don't get me wrong, it can be great to connect with the person who has done what you want to do. Given how easy it is to get information about other people's lives and reach out, it would be silly not to use them as benchmarks to map out your own path to success, and have confidence that things are going to work out as planned. If it happened to them, then it's possible for you too, right?

The Internet Blackhole

But beware of the trap that exists in this amplified, continual tirade of information available at your fingertips. I'm sure at some point, we've all been suckered into what I like to call the internet blackhole. Have you ever logged into your computer to do something, and all of a sudden you 'wake up', and find yourself on Facebook (or some other social media outlet), and over an hour has passed since you first sat down? Or was that two hours ago? But I guess you know that your best friend's cousins wife and younger sister are having a fight, and also that Neiman Marcus is having a sale on shoes, so it hasn't been a complete waste of time. But you can't remember why you sat down in front of the computer in the first place. Oh look, Beyonce has a new album out…

Mayday! Call in the troops, you've fallen into the internet blackhole!

I wouldn't beat yourself up if you've found this happening. The name of the game in advertising, marketing and PR is to keep you engaged as much as possible. Through the use of smart analytics that track your purchasing behavior and habits, your smart computer has become very savvy in finding out what you like. By using this knowledge, they deploy sneaky tactics to keep you watching. Because while you are engaged and looking, you're more likely to buy something, and this means The Other Guys will continue to be successful.

The Other Guys

Maybe you are wondering who The Other Guys are. Have you ever seen the comedy action film, *'The Other Guys',* with those two policemen partners in it, played by Mark Wahlburg and Will Ferrell? Okay - so I'm not talking about *those guys.* I'm talking about **The Other Guys.** I've also referred to The Other Guys guys as *The Flight Crew* a little earlier on.

They are the guys who are completely invested in their own journey and path to greatness. **The Other Guys** are typically the ones who have spent their hard earned money on advertising, PR and social media in order to have you watching them or buying their creations. The Other Guys are *rarely* in the Internet black hole, because in order for **The Other Guys** to be known as **The Other Guys,** they can't afford to fall in there.

Time is their greatest asset, and that time is better allocated on **The Other Guys** creating things in their relevant industries that position them to be better than they were before. So much work, time, energy, and passion is spent on creating new work. After partnering their creations with PR/advertising campaigns, it keeps them at the top of their field with all of the top **Other Guys** in **The Other Guys**. Get it? Because if you do, and you put this knowledge into practice in your own life in real time, then I'd be willing to bet my money on guaranteeing your success in whatever you decide to do - not only in the area of your health and fitness!

I was having dinner with a friend a few nights ago, and she expressed some disappointment about another mutual friend of ours that never seemed to like any of her pictures on Facebook. She felt it was selfish on his part, because she was always liking his posts and felt the favor was never returned. However, the person she is referring to is starting to become very successful in his industry. There have been multiple people that have expressed disappointment in his inability to take an interest in people's lives outside of his own.

While there may be some truth to that, the success that has come about in his life illustrates to me that he is living his passion and is **so invested in his own journey to greatness** that he doesn't really watch what anybody else is doing. Perhaps it seems selfish to some; which in some manner it is. But arguably, it's selfish in the same way that putting on your own oxygen mask **first** before assisting others in the event of an airplane crash is selfish.

So it begs to question: Are his actions selfish, or is it an action or **jump** that exercises and illustrates the ultimate act of self care and self worth? Is it blind selfishness, or is it an effort to step into his own greatness so he can be in a better place to help her if she ever asked; in an astronomically better way in the future than liking a few of her pictures could ever do?

It's a matter of opinion, but I would argue that if he was spending time on the internet, (falling into blackholes to watch and like other peoples pictures all of the time) he wouldn't be a member of **The Other Guys.**

Your Race Alone

With all of this being said, even the most successful of people can find themselves comparing themselves to others. While this is a good motivator for some, it is in fact an incredibly unfair comparison. Often this comparison comes at the expense of your happiness, progression, and your journey to your **Fitness Utopia.**

This is because no other person has lived your life, and has walked your path. To compare yourself to another, (even if you are in the same industry, and have been in it for the same amount of time), is not a fair comparison at all. If you have been diligent in exercises in self worth, my bet is that you understand there is room for everyone's authentic individual greatness.

Rest assured that when you are true to yourself, and you create in a manner that reflects your own special expression and flavor, **no one** can come close to your greatness. To compare yourself to someone else is disrespectful of your own strengths and infinite worth. You are incomparable, and as original as your fingerprint!

For example, it's no secret that there are millions of self help books out there in the cosmos, as well as books on working out and health and fitness. But, if I let that hinder me, thinking that it's all been done before, you wouldn't be sitting here reading this book. Because the truth is, no one can write like me. Because they are not me!

By the same token, have confidence that what exists within you is so original and so amazing! To have the courage to tap into that greatness, and share your gifts with the world is *exactly* what you were put on Earth to do. Shine bright like the diamond you are! Because in taking a chance, to **jump**, to shine bright in the way *that only you can,* gives permission (and hope to others), that it is okay to light up their own candles and rise up too.

Your race means working hard to better yourself in the most fearless way possible, despite what others are doing, or whether anyone has done what you have done before. Also, what you are often comparing your real self to is someone else's highlight reel: complete with the Valencia filter. And #DuhBecky, everyone looks amazing in a Valencia filter!

The Mind Diet Mental Moves

On Staying In The Zone and Staying In Your Lane

Mental will is a muscle that needs exercise, just like the muscles of the body.
Lynn Jennings, American Long Distance Runner

So how do we train our minds to focus on our own journey? Just like a muscle, (and similar to most of the moves I have mentioned in the toolbox of **The Mind Diet)** mental moves in focus should be added into your plan regularly. Listed below are some of my favorite exercises in building focus, concentration and willpower. You can apply these benefits to staying on track for your nutrition plan, following a workout, planning your schedule (or even in the area of your career, spirituality or relationships).

Focus Bulk

Whenever you are trying to train your mind to focus, it's always advisable to start small. Similar to someone starting as a beginner on a weightlifting program, (beginning with a lighter weight, staying consistent and progressing from there) the focus bulk works in line with these principles. You begin with a small amount of focus on incidental things for small periods of time, and then increase gradually. Because if you cant be trusted with the small stuff, how can you succeed with the big stuff?

I build my focus with my cat, Gandalf. I'm not sure how this happened, but he is convinced he is a dog, and one of his favorite games is to play fetch. Each day, he would bring his toy mouse over and drop it by my feet as a signal to ask me to play. I would find myself tossing it a few times, then wandering off after two or three minutes… distracted. Usually the phone would ring, or I'd think about food, or things I might have had to do that day.

But I decided as a responsibility to him and also to build my focus, I would play everyday with him starting with five minute rounds. This meant if I decided to play, I was locked in for five minutes and had to commit for the entire time. So I set my timer, and focused completely on him and our playtime. This meant no phones, no computers, no snacks, no yoga, and no TV at the same time. Just Gandalf and I, his toy mouse, and playtime.

As you can imagine at the beginning, it felt like a long, long time before the 5 minute timer went off. Can you imagine? Now I'm up to 15 minute intervals everyday, usually twice a day. You can imagine how ecstatic he is. It has been a great way for me to bond with him. Being completely present (wherever you are) can add color and flavor to everyday moments in our lives that so many of us have forgotten about.

Meditation

There is so much information out there in the cosmos that

teaches you how to meditate. If you've never tried it, today is the day to begin. Because basically, our mind is a wild and ratchet creature if we let it be one.

I once heard a monk call the human mind a monkey mind. He believes when the mind is busy, it is a monkey mind, thinking this thing or that, without discipline. The solution was not to yell, and scream, and get frustrated. That would just encourage the monkey mind to keep on being ratchet and out of control. Instead, the monkey mind needed a job. When beginning meditation instead, you simply ask the monkey mind to sit still. Then, with your eyes closed, focus on a chosen point in your head. I always like to think of a flickering candle that gets smaller when I breathe in, and larger when I breathe out.

Start small, just like doing the Focus Bulk. Trust me, if you are doing this for the first time, five minutes will seem like an eternity! If you have chosen this as one of your **Mind Diet Mental Moves**, schedule them accordingly into your planner, with your forecasted increase in meditation time as the weeks progress.

Memorization moves

There are many different ways to learn how to memorize things. One of my favorite methods is memorization by association of a familiar journey.

For example, my route to my gym is the same. I know each street post I pass (and also other landmarks that I see along the way). The Starbucks, The Ralph's Supermarket, a yoga studio and a popular nightclub. If I am wanting to learn something, I endow each street post (and landmark) with the new information I am wanting to learn. I then practice this association in my head. Each day when I go to the gym, I say each association out loud when I pass each street post and landmark. It's amazing what you can memorize by doing this!

Learn To Listen

As they say, two ears and one mouth means you should be listening twice as much as you're talking. Besides, have you ever spent time with someone that doesn't stop talking? You know, a "Chatty Cathy?" Maybe it's the introvert in me coming out, but whenever I'm with a Chatty Cathy, I quickly find myself getting tired. It's absolutely exhausting if a conversation is one sided all of the time. Sharing your ideas and contributing in a conversation by talking is obviously necessary in the game of human interaction. But if you're doing more talking than listening, I believe you're missing out on the full extent of one of life's greatest gifts: genuine human connection, or to put it another way, human love. If you find you are lacking depth in your relationships or interactions, and you want to change this, the next time you interact with someone, stay quiet and listen to them. Truly listen to them, and be interested in their stories, the way you would want people to listen to you. I would say part of the reason I have a very strong relationship with my clients is because I practice this mental move every day. Small details remembered about a person's life. Paired with genuine interest, love and care can change the depth of a relationship. And you learn so much more! So zip it!

No Gossip Zone/No Negativity Zone

I'll be the first person to admit that this **mental move** is hard for me. This year, it was my new years resolution that I wouldn't gossip about anyone, and I would steer clear of negativity and toxicity at all costs.

Although it hasn't been perfect, simply having the intention as my resolution has helped me to identify gossip and negativity when it starts, or whenever it's around me. It's like a red flag that mentally goes up in my mind whenever toxicity is present. From there, I am able to choose how to respond: whether I end the conversation in question, change the subject completely or vocalize my boundary of not wanting to contribute or be involved in this perceived toxicity.

To complete this mental move, schedule it into your calendar for one day. Then on that day, commit to only saying positive and cheerful things, and choose only to be a part of situations and events that elevate you.

What do you discover? When I first started, I found it hard to talk about anything. Because in doing this, I soon realized most of the things that I talked about had a negative connotation to it. In time however, I chose to put cheerful things in that space. You don't need to be a rocket scientist to know how much better that is for your health, your mindset and your life.

The Lesson

If you're watching other people race, that means you're there standing still. Make moves!

Chapter 13

Finish What You Started

Done is better than good.
- Elizabeth Gilbert

Imagine working very hard on your journey to your **Fitness Utopia**, and giving it your very best. Doing all of the challenging jumps necessary to create the space to live as your best self. But at the very last moment, you choose not to take the last jump. Or not take it **yet**... and that yet continues on for the rest of your days on Earth. The final jump that would solidify the completion of your trip, and define your arrival at your **Fitness Utopia**. Call it procrastination, call it self sabotage, call it being a perfectionist. Whatever the reasons are behind it are, not taking this final jump essentially means you did not finish what you started.

The Unlikely Procrastinator

When you think of a chronic procrastinator, does a perfectionist come to mind? To me, they seem like mutually exclusive attributes. Because generally speaking, when one thinks of a procrastinator, someone super lazy might come to mind. There is another type of chronic procrastinator in this world however, and this procrastinator looks very different to the one I'm referring to above.

The procrastinator I am talking about is always super busy starting big projects. Creating this thing or that, half projects and tasks up in the air, juggling with loads of potential like a professional juggling act you might otherwise see at the circus.

But this procrastinator has nothing too concrete to show for it. If you are this kind of procrastinator, you are always teetering for far too long on your mountains edge, or preparing yourself to stand on multiple mountain tops all at the same time, and never, ever jumping. And as we know, if we don't **jump**, nothing gets done. And if nothing gets done… nothing gets changed.

Although these procrastinators look different to each other, the reason each type of person is a chronic procrastinator begins from similar root causes in self worth, fear of failure, analysis paralysis, and fear of success. Because if it's not done, you haven't failed yet. Does this resonate with you?

> **People don't want to have their ability judged, they'd rather have their effort judged.**
>
> **- Joseph Ferrari, Professor Psychology De Paul University**

Prolonging completion of a task or project could be one way of avoiding the fear of being harshly evaluated. Do you remember my own example of self sabotage when doing my first fitness competition? I had been prepping fantastically for the **when** I had set for myself in five solid months. I was flying across the country to be evaluated for my work for the first time. Up until that point, I was communicating with my coaches online, and they were assessing me on my effort to complete my workouts, and prepare my meals properly. But once I flew over there, they would be judging me in person, and with the view I was presenting my completed work. This ultimately meant that I might fail. And because I was so afraid to fail and deep down, did not think I had any business doing what I was doing, I sabotaged my own preparation.

There is a book called *'Still Procrastinating: The No Regrets Guide to Getting It Done'*, by Joseph Ferrari. His research illustrates that nearly a quarter of adults around the world are chronic procrastinators, and these same people are more often that not also defined as perfectionists. So if you're like me (and you've found yourself habitually part of this quarter population in areas of your life), know that it's a fairly common issue to have. That doesn't mean it's OK though! It simply means that if you're now aware that you're hanging out with some of the other birds in *Fitness Mediocrity Land*, you have the choice to do something about it. By using the principles in **The Mind**

Diet, you can choose to create a new story and change the course of your future. By making the choice to **jump**, you are creating the opportunity to live your life at your healthiest and highest capacity. How cool is that?!

In Chapter 6, we discussed the importance for becoming BFF's with failure. Becoming BFF's with failure is not only for those **jumps** that you'll need to move forward, but also for that final BIG **jump** you'll need to finish what you started. The last leap to arrive at your individually and fantastically defined **Fitness Utopia.**

Every jump is **so important**, and every jump needed to happen to get you to where you are today. (And so did every perceived failure too.) This includes the last jump too, friends! The jump that shows that you left the ground, reached for the beam and made it to your final stop, even if it took you a few attempts.

Have you ever watched the show *"American Ninja Warrior?"* The contestants are timed as they run through many challenging obstacles to reach a final warped wall. This wall is a fourteen foot vertical climb that's curved at the ends. The contestant has to run all the way up the wall and climb over the top to hit the red button. Hitting the red button signifies they have completed the whole challenge. Depending on their time to completion, they will then move onto the next round of competition.

Each contestant has three chances to make it up the warped wall before they are disqualified from the competition. Can you imagine if one of the contestants got as far as the warped wall, through all of those challenging initial obstacles, and at this final moment:

- They stand and stare at the wall, frozen in place. They try to work out a strategy to get up the wall, but do not make the qualifying time because they were too busy deciding on their strategy.

- They make one attempt but do not make it up to the top to the red button. They decide to not try again (even though there are two other chances available).

- They decided it was altogether too difficult, so throw it into the "too hard basket", and walk off without even attempting once.

If any of these things listed above were to happen on national television, the contestant would be the talk of the town. They would look absolutely bat shit crazy. However, so many of us do these **exact things** in our own lives! It's pure madness when you think about it. You've put in so much effort already. So why not get your reward from it?

If you have been doing **The Mind Diet Mental Moves** with diligence, you'll have a very clear idea of what your **Fitness Utopia** looks like, and you'll be exercising your scheduled combination of customized mental moves that work on dealing with issues in fear of failure, self worth, and ruminating tendencies.

I've mentioned it before, but it's worth saying again: The first way to change where you are going is to accept, and take responsibility for where you are. So, using the table on the following page, drink your honesty serum, and list as the events where you find yourself chronically procrastinating.

	PROCRASTINATION EVENT	WHY	ACTION OF CHANGE	WHEN (LITTLE D)
1				
2				
3				

Are you surprised at what you wrote down? While some things are not meant to be finished, is there something listed which completing would work in line with taking that last jump to arrive at your **Fitness Utopia**? If you have been honest with your list, there should be a few tasks that were uncompleted which can account for you not reaching your destination previously.

If you're a chronic procrastinator like I am, you must love thinking of the big picture. But we get so caught up in the big picture (or the end goal), that we end up not executing the detailed jumps or steps we need to take to make our big picture a reality. Both are important for success. Without a solid understanding of each, you'll either walk through each step of life not knowing where you are going or why; or you'll know where you're going, but have no idea on how to get there.

As In Fitness, So In Life

Based on what I have learned in the gym, I have chosen to

create a new story in my own life. You see, I had been stuck in a habit where I'd start many big tasks with much enthusiasm, but not finish them. The root cause was working through issues in my fear of failure. I always had in the back of my mind that I hadn't finished, so essentially hadn't failed. But of course, when doing this for every big task, nothing was finished, and I definitely didn't succeed either - and therefore, ended up failing by default. It took me a long time to accept, and see this for what it was. But simply recognizing why this was happening, forgiving myself, and through using **The Mind Diet** principles, I began to make the changes necessary to create a new reality.

This book is my own challenge to solidify instilling this new story. That yes, I've started many things that I haven't finished, and I've failed by default. But those failures woke me up to the lessons I needed to execute in self care and self worth. It taught me that I needed to change my behavior, habits and thoughts if I wanted to step into my greatness, and share this gift with the world. To share this gift and help you rise into your healthiest and best self, I needed to become BFF's with my fear of failure. I needed to finish what I started. I needed to **jump!**

If you are currently going through some big changes, I understand so clearly what this feeling is like. I've been successful in making my **Fitness Utopia** a reality. But now it's time to take my next level to the next level by creating a **Utopia of Greatness**. Intention to live as my best self in the areas of health, career, relationships, and spirituality.

The Mind Diet is my **jump.** I've jumped, (despite not knowing what would happen), but having a sense that the un-comfortability of pushing past my fear of failure cannot compare to the joy that is coming. The health of people I could change, despite never having met them. The people who I can help grow into their best selves, so they can help others from a place of their own individual greatness. And of course, it might fail. But even if I don't sell a single book, I've grown so much in this process, that it's been a complete win for me anyway.

You are literally bound my nothing but the limits you have chosen in your mind (and the limits in other people's minds too, if you choose.) It may take a few failed jumps, or multiple jumps to arrive at your **Fitness Utopia**... and/or your

Utopia of Greatness.

But every time you begin again, you are creating a momentum that propels you forward. With the experience of the past, you can begin again, this time more intelligently. You may not get there as fast as you may have liked, or as fast as your co-worker, or friend, or family member has wanted you to. But trust that just like in health and fitness, your body knows what to do! It is an exquisite creation (and a privilege to operate), because it's your vehicle to your highest self. Within it, houses **all of the tools you need**. Once you really see the value of your body (and the legitimate greatness that exists within you), it is so easy to treat it with the utmost respect and love.

Fitness has taught me priceless lessons about redefining my own limits, my own habits, and showing me exactly what has been holding me back from sharing my gifts with the world. So maybe you've been a chronic procrastinator in your health and life; or you are dealing with issues in self worth, confidence, perceived failure, or your fear of it. You've made some mistakes. But so what? With **The Mind Diet's** mental moves and lessons, I truly hope it teaches you that at any moment, wherever you are: **you can choose** to write a new story, and become who you know (and I know) that you can be. And I hope you've learned it's okay to make a mistake, and it's okay to fail! It's okay to give something an honest go and for it not to turn out the way you wanted. Because instead, I'll bet you'll have come away with the lesson on how to begin again with new information, and a better chance to succeed.

This is true not only for fitness and health, but all aspects of your life: career, spirituality and relationships. If you're scared about what people might think or say if you "fail" - rest easy knowing that while they are watching, they are not invested in their own race. By focusing on you, they are wasting their own valuable time (and unfortunately, their entire lives away), which actually results in them becoming bigger failures than they believe you to be. So in essence, are any attempts you make really a failure?

When things don't work out how I had envisioned, I'd always find that after a little time had passed I would see why my path needed to change. To date, every no has always led me to a bigger yes down the road. I never know the exact timing of it, but armed with my **faith muscle ups**, I have never been disappointed with the growth and elevation that has resulted in my life because of any of my "failures". In times of challenge, your mental moves will help to remind you of these things, and have you moving forward, despite the un-comfortability and the fear that plagues the road to your **Fitness Utopia**.

Without experiencing these issues of chronic procrastination, self sabotage, issues in self worth, anxiety, failure (and my fear of it), I wouldn't be sitting here writing this book (with the experience that I needed), to then be able to empathize and share with you the steps to break these habits and step into your own greatness. I feel honored to share this gift with you! If **The Mind Diet** were to help one person rise into their greatness, it would make everything I dealt with (to be armed with the wisdom to write this book), completely worth it!

My completion of **The Mind Diet** marks my final jump to create a new story in my career. A story where I finish what I start. A story where I take my jumps all the way to the finish line. A true story, where I rose up out of failure after failure, and how I did it. A story that ends with a book that may not be perfect, but if you're reading it right now, that means I've jumped, and it's done. Meet me out on the beam!

The Lesson

Finish what you started and get what you ran all that way for.

#YouAreWorthIt

Chapter 14

Give It Away

I hope the fruits of my labor are ripe for many generations to come.
- Donovan Nichols

Anywhere worth going is never worth it in the end if you can't share it with the ones you love. One of the most frustrating things for me as a fitness professional is wanting to share what I've learned with people who I believe I can help. Upon working with them, however, I see that they are not yet in the mindset needed to make the changes necessary for their goals to manifest.

You see, **The Mind Diet** is only successful if you want it to be. If you believe in your heart that you can change, and you feel you are deserving of this change. Perhaps you may not believe it completely at this moment, and this is why you're here. If you are committed to doing your **mental moves** however, then I have the utmost confidence that you will start to believe with 100% certainty that you can change, and in time, create the space for amazing transformations to occur.

Everyone is on their own journey in this lifetime, walking and learning their own lessons at their own individual pace. As much as you wish, argue or demand, you can't save people, or force them to live at your pace, or in the same way that you do.

But it is your duty on this Earth to pass on what you know to others who are ready to learn, so you may rise together. If you've made the **jumps** needed and have arrived at your **Fitness Utopia**, I'll bet you've had some help along the way from others that were already on the beam. They threw you a few seeds, and you used this as fuel to fire your own journey to success. Congratulations! It's now time to turn around and pass it on.

It's the attribute of those living in their own greatness to assist those that are ready to make the **jump** (in whatever manner is necessary) to get them out onto the beam, where the real party is at!

Since letting go of toxicity, and creating the space for greatness to occur, I have had some **truly exquisite individuals** enter my life; that in time, have assisted me in my own growth, transformation and elevation, for which I will be forever grateful.

In the spirit of passing on what I know, **The Mind Diet** is my gift to you, when you're ready to walk the path. *The Flight Crew* wants you out on the beam… but only you can jump for yourself.

And I truly hope you do.

See you there!

ACKNOWLEDGMENTS

Any race to greatness is never run alone. Without the encouragement, presence, and advice of the following individuals, I doubt this book would even exist today!

In no particular order, thank you to Tracy Poust, (Writer/Executive Producer *Will and Grace, Ugly Betty*) for your encouragement and positivity on overcoming my fears, and getting my book out there to the world!

To my long time friend Paul 'The Mauler' Lazenby (Pro Wrestler, Author, *When We Were Bouncers*), whose copywriting skills are surprisingly astute considering the amount of punches he's taken to the face in his lifetime.

To Tahndi Campbell, (Lionsgate Entertainment) for your friendship, laughs, encouragement and advice on the final edit of *The Mind Diet*; and also for taking a chance on me for The BeFiT Channel!

To Dr. Mike Dow (NY Times Best Selling Author, *The Brain Fog Fix*), I'm blessed to have had you around to pick your brain, given you have walked the path before with much success. Thank you for your tips!

To Lauren Jones and Nicole Wool (Jones Social PR), for your friendship, advice, and assistance in my LA chapter.

To Luke Milton (Training Mate), your gym pulled me out of the biggest depression of my lifetime, and gave me a platform to reach the biggest game players in Los Angeles, doing exactly what I do best: teaching and inspiring through health and fitness. Thank you!

To the many physiques I've had the pleasure of transforming over the years: thank you ALL for trusting me with your bodies, and your lives. It's been a blessing to guide and run alongside you and watch as each person's journey unfolds. Without you guys, this book wouldn't exist!

And to all the people along the way who hurt me, lied to me, betrayed me, or broke me. You taught me so much more than you could ever have taken from me. You are my greatest teachers. Thank you.

ABOUT THE AUTHOR

Edwina Cheer is an Australian Celebrity Sports Nutritionist, Personal Trainer, Fitness Model and Group Fitness Instructor based in Los Angeles, California.

She is a Certified Strength & Conditioning Coach (CSCS/NSCA). She aspires to complete her Doctorate in Physical Therapy (DPT) in 2021 and assists other licensed Physical Therapists on a regular basis at The UCLA Ronald Reagan Center.

She has worked in various capacities with celebrity clients Quinton "Rampage" Jackson, Jonathan Bennett, Jesse Metcalfe, Arianny Celeste, Allen Leech, Tom Lenk, and a host of other title MMA fighters, and Australian public figures.

She is a Resident Contributor of the BeFit Channel of Lionsgate Entertainment, which currently boasts the largest subscriber base for fitness content on YouTube. Recent TV appearances include a featured segment on ABC7 with fitness icon Jackie Warner and Health Host Lori Corbin.

She specializes in weight-loss, sports nutrition through scientific programming, macronutrient counting and workouts of high intensity. She enjoys interacting with her loyal following on social media where much of her fitness videos & nutrition advice is showcased.

Connect with her here:
Twitter: twitter.com/eddsthetics
Instagram: instagram.com/eddsthetics
Facebook: facebook.com/eddsthetics
Snapchat: @eddsthetics

48072500R00172

Made in the USA
San Bernardino, CA
15 April 2017